MW00776211

Vida y Hacienda

The Life and Legacy
of Dr. Pedro Albizu Campos

Andre Lee Muñiz

Remembering Don Pedro, 2022

Vida y Hacienda:
The Life and Legacy of
Dr. Pedro Albizu Campos

Andre Lee Muñiz

Cover Art: Yasmín Hernández
(E-mail: YasminHernandezArt@gmail.com)

Cover Design: Brandon Chacon
(E-mail: BrandonChacon96@gmail.com)

© Andre Lee Muniz
© Remembering Don Pedro
E-mail: RememberingDonPedro@gmail.com

Published July 14, 2022
ISBN: 978-0-578-29275-5

BIOGRAPHY — HISTORY — PUERTO RICO

This book is a work of dedication

...a promise i made
to my father, from the heart,
fourteen years ago

Acknowledgements

Acknowledgements first go to my ancestors, especially my father, Stanley Muñiz, who this book is dedicated to. I also give special thanks to my mother, Daisy Muñiz, for carrying and delivering me here, and to the rest of my large family for providing a strong foundation to grow on.

As a lover of Puerto Rican history, I give thanks to those historical giants that rightfully fill the pages in the books about our nation, and to the masses of people without which our nation and its history wouldn't exist.

I also give thanks to:

Carmen Mojica for making a father and a better person out of me, and for giving me insight into how to influence change from the source. Samuel Sanchez for developing a personal relationship with me as a father figure and mentor during the most challenging time of my life. Yasmín Hernández for understanding and supporting the vision I had for my work around Don Pedro and creating the cover art to this book. Imani Nuñez for also supporting me since the beginning and designing the first set of logos for Remembering Don Pedro. Hiram Rivera Marcano for providing honest and thoughtful feedback that challenged my inner voice. Daniel Morales-Armstrong for also giving feedback that proved to be greatly helpful in the editing of this book. My religious elders for providing me the space and support to connect to the world in a more profound and purposeful way. Everyone I have met and interacted with thanks to my project, *Remembering Don Pedro*, for returning the energy I put into it. You, the reader, for feeling this book of mine was worth engaging with.

Preface

I

A few months before my father Stanley Muñiz passed away in 2007, one week after my 21st birthday, I shared a special moment with him. It was around the time when my passion for studying Puerto Rican history became a central part of my life, and when my father's health complications began pointing towards what eventually came to manifest. In that moment, I found myself walking into his room, sitting down beside him, and pouring out things I was holding in my heart.

I told him how much he meant to me. I told him that I didn't know what was going to happen, and that I loved him. I told him that I didn't know why I was saying what I was saying, but that I knew I had to say it. I also told him that I was going to write books one day, and that my first book would be dedicated to him.

At the time, I was entering my first year at NYU. Only two years removed from the struggling high school student that I was, nothing about me suggested I would write anything serious outside of those assignments connected to my coursework. As they usually do, experiences and circumstances eventually opened the door to new possibilities. As I completed my degrees at NYU, I also developed an intense personal study of Puerto Rican history, which was a key part of how I coped with my father's transition.

II

I began to walk the path to becoming an author in 2013. By that time, I had already begun practicing the craft of writing by creating pamphlets on figures and topics in Puerto Rican history out of my desire to share what I was learning with friends. But, more importantly, two things coincided that year that I can say put me on my path in a practical way. First, I worked briefly at the Center for Puerto Rican Studies (CENTRO) Library and Archives at Hunter College. Second, I began writing for the online Boricua Diaspora publication *La Respuesta* magazine, of which I soon became the NYC Regional Editor.

At CENTRO, my personal drive to continue studying Puerto Rican history meant that I made time in my off-hours to tap into their tremendous wealth of resources. Among other topics, this is when I truly began to research the life of Dr. Pedro Albizu Campos. Having access to scans of newspapers from his era, the oral history conducted with Ruth Reynolds, a white anti-imperialist that became his close friend and supporter, and more, I was almost overwhelmed with research material. It wasn't long before I began to consider the idea of writing a book on Don Pedro. I even developed detailed outlines that I used to create the book in your hands.

With *La Respuesta* magazine, I was challenged to develop my writing through close collaboration with other Boricua writers and editors. In my three years working with the publication, I began to identify as a writer. It also provided me the personally meaningful opportunity to write more on Don Pedro to an interested audience.

In the years after I stopped working with *La Respuesta* magazine in 2016, I continued to study Puerto Rican history, though at a different pace than I had in the past. And then, in 2020, we were hit with a global pandemic.

III

As was the case for many people, the global pandemic provided me with more time to be with my family, and to start new projects or continue work on old ones. In my case, I decided to revisit the research and draft material

I had collected over the years in my work around Don Pedro. With my dream being to write a book about him one day, I decided to first create the website *RememberingDonPedro.com* as a way to get the creative juices flowing in that direction.

The purpose behind the website was and is to provide an online history of Don Pedro, a single site of reference for people interested in learning about the life of Don Pedro from his birth to his transition to the spirit world. Presenting his history first through the website, my intent was to increase free access to his important story to the general public.

Marisa Rosado's 1992 Spanish-language biography on Don Pedro—Pedro Albizu Campos: Las Llamas de la Aurora, Acercamiento a su Biografía— served as an indispensable reference. My hope is that this book allows English-language audiences to learn about the life and legacy of one of the most important figures in Puerto Rico's history that has, until now, been more accessible to Spanish-language readers.

By offering a wider and at times more detailed focus, I hope that this book can serve as a valuable complement to the biography on Don Pedro written by Federico Ribes Tovar—Albizu Campos: Puerto Rican Revolutionary—that is available in English. Ribes Tovar's book, popular among English-language readers, is a translation from its original Spanish printing, making this book the first biography on Don Pedro to be written in English, an intimidating fact and significant responsibility I do not take lightly.

Though having the university training to approach this book from an academic perspective, I attempted to strike a balance between writing and organizing it in a way that is accessible to a more general audience, while also providing a level of detail beneficial to scholars of Puerto Rican history.

The book is organized into seven major time periods, and, with some exceptions, all chapters were kept to 3-5 pages. This was done for two reasons—to provide general readers an historical account that can be engaged with relative ease, and to create a resource for schools, book clubs, workshops, learning circles, and other initiatives able to raise awareness around Don Pedro and Puerto Rican history.

IV

When I was young my father, a life-long *independentista*, used to ask me, "When are you going to learn your history? When are you going to learn about Don Pedro?" It wasn't until he transitioned that I took it upon myself to learn about our repressed history. This is the book I wish was available to me when I was young and learning about my nation's history.

Andre Lee Muñiz
The Bronx, NY

Introduction

In any organization with a clearly defined set of values, it is important that members see leaders embodying and maintaining integrity to those very values. More than a set of values to be held, the *Partido Nacionalista de Puerto Rico* required/requires an oath of those wishing to join its ranks, a swearing of one's willingness to sacrifice their life and property—*vida y hacienda*—to the struggle for independence. As the Party's de facto leader from 1930 until his transition in 1965, Dr. Pedro Albizu Campos undeniably embodied the fulfillment of this oath.

Of course, for those picking up this book and just beginning to learn about Don Pedro, a brief introduction is in order.

Born of an extra-marital affair in the 1890s, Don Pedro was raised by his maternal family in a neighborhood of Ponce founded by formerly enslaved people of African descent. Choosing to start school at age 12, he excelled as a student and graduated high school as class president seven years later. Earning a scholarship to continue his studies in the United States, he eventually became the first Puerto Rican to graduate from Harvard University and Harvard Law School. While at Harvard, he also was an active student activist and organizer, earned a commission as an infantry officer in the U.S. Army, and developed fluency in seven languages beyond his native Spanish. Turning down a number of job offers upon completing his studies he decided to return to Puerto Rico in 1921 and work as a lawyer in defense of the poor.

Once back in Puerto Rico, Don Pedro married and eventually fathered four children, one outside of his marriage. Becoming an active independence supporter, he quickly emerged as a prominent leader and was elected president of the Nationalist Party in 1930. He transformed the Party into a significant force seeking to secure Puerto Rico's sovereignty as a nation. Due to the undeniable success he had in organizing the Party throughout Puerto Rico, he was targeted with surveillance and persecution by the U.S. and colonial governments. Between the years 1936, when he was convicted and imprisoned for the first time, and 1965, when he passed away, he spent two and a half decades in prison or exile. His physical death was a direct result of the conditions of his imprisonment, especially from those years in which he was intentionally targeted with lethal amounts of radiation.

Don Pedro's life and legacy earned him a place in Puerto Rico's history as a significant and important figure. Historians and individuals from a wide range of backgrounds have kept his legacy alive in diverse ways. Owing to Puerto Rico's continued status as a colonial territory, such efforts have been undertaken with great passion and often with considerable personal sacrifice. Unfortunately for English-language readers, most of the written work about Don Pedro has been done in Spanish. This book was created with the intention of providing English-language readers a valuable resource for learning about Don Pedro.

I have organized this book into thirty-eight chapters across seven major time periods in Don Pedro's life. The first two periods—*Roots and Childhood* and *University Experience*—provide a foundational view of Don Pedro's youth, educational experiences, travels, and influences. The next three— *Early Professional Life*, *First Nationalist Party Era*, and *10 Years Of Exile*— offer a detailed look at his rise as a prominent *independentista*, his organizing in Puerto Rico and beyond, and the impact of his challenges to the colonial regime. The final two periods—*Second Nationalist Party Era* and *Final Years and Legacy*—cover Don Pedro's return to the island after his exile, the final years of his independence organizing, his death, and the ways his legacy has been kept alive.

With this book there has been an attempt at balancing depth and breadth, leaning more on the side of the latter in order to cover a wide range of Don Pedro's life. While my primary goal was to simply fill the gap existing for English-language readers by drawing from the Spanish-language record, I also offer new scholarship by incorporating seldom used references and expanding on lesser-discussed topics. My hope is that readers will use this book as a starting point for developing further writings in English on Don Pedro that expand on the many interesting and historically important aspects of his life.

One of the lesser-discussed topics this book provides insight into is his military experience. What exactly was he exposed to during his military education in the Harvard R.O.T.C. program? If R.O.T.C. programs extend a commission as an officer to its graduates, why was Don Pedro sent to Puerto Rico by the U.S. Army as a Private? What was Don Pedro doing in Puerto Rico during his service with the U.S. Army?

Another topic covered in this book, which is rarely mentioned in both English- and Spanish-language texts, is Don Pedro's consistent advocacy to hold a constitutional convention in Puerto Rico. Most texts which discuss Don Pedro's activities in 1936 highlight his trial for seditious conspiracy and eventual imprisonment. Completely overlooked is the call he made, while on trial, to bring the leaders of all political parties together in a convention where they would declare Puerto Rico's independence as a nation and begin the process of determining how to move forward as a country and what international relations it would have with the U.S. and the rest of the world. What makes this call for a constitutional convention so incredible is the fact that it received widespread support across Puerto Rican society, even from statehood supporters, and that it was a goal of Don Pedro's from the very beginning of his political career.

Two other lesser-discussed topics detailed in this book include the infamous Gag Law and Don Pedro's wife, Doña Laura. The Gag Law was designed to repress all political dissent to such an extreme level that it denied individuals their right to freedom of speech, assembly, the press, and more. The law incarcerated individuals for giving speeches, writing articles, and even for clapping at political events and leaving flowers at the graves of nationalists. As said in the title of the chapter devoted to it, it is *A Law And Era To Be Remembered* because of the influence it had on attitudes towards pro-independence sentiment and leaders, and more.

Dr. Laura Meneses de Albizu Campos is so often written off simply as Don Pedro's wife. In actuality, she did a tremendous amount of work internationally in support of Puerto Rico's independence. She was also a key figure in the work to free Don Pedro and all other imprisoned members of the Nationalist Party throughout the years, beginning in 1936. As the first Latin American woman to be accepted into Harvard University, she entered its women's division, Radcliffe College, already having a doctoral degree from her native Peru. By devoting a chapter to Doña Laura, I hope to influence efforts to honor her as a pioneer in her own right and not simply as Don Pedro's wife.

So much can be written about Don Pedro, a historical figure considered controversial by some, but admired and respected by even more. This controversy, of course, stems from the fact that he lived in opposition to the colonial rule of Puerto Rico by the U.S. government, which continues today. The day Puerto Rico becomes an independent nation, Don Pedro will certainly take his rightful place as a revered national hero and icon, for he lived and gave his life in the service of one thing: the emergence of the nation of Puerto Rico among the other free nations of the world.

"The case of your father is an extraordinary case: a young man, full of life, endowed with the faculties and virtues that can make him happy and elevate him high above mediocrity, and who, when seeing the exploitation and crime of which his people are victim, rebels against injustice, sacrifices his well-being, his genius, frustrates his prospects that are not for the good of his people, sacrifices his freedom and finally allows him to be murdered for leaving his people a weapon to defend themselves, That is your father."

Dr. Laura Meneses de Albizu Campos
(Letter to daughter Laura Esperanza, Mexico 1957)

Dr. Pedro Albizu Campos with his wife and their three children, Pedro, Rosa Emilia, and Laura Esperanza

Table Of Contents

List Of Tables

A Note On Sources

The *References* section (p. 212) has the full list of works referenced in the development of this book. Many of the chapters in this book were originally posts on RememberingDonPedro.com. More specific citations were added for this book as endnotes. These endnotes are on the following pages:

First Period — Roots and Childhood

Chapter 1: National Identity And El Grito De Lares

Borikén

The story of humans in the Caribbean islands is said to begin around the year 4000B.C. and from two primary directions, the Yucatán to the west and Northeastern South America to the south. Over the next few thousand years, waves of people made their way across the Caribbean islands, inevitably coming into contact and interacting with each other. The earliest people to settle the islands were stone-age hunter-gatherers, whereas later settlers were agriculturalists and producers of ceramics.

Academics point to the period between 600A.D. and 1200A.D. as when many of the societies that had been established began to develop the complex social and political structures observed by Europeans in 1492. While multiple cultural groups lived in the Caribbean, one eventually spanned across a significant portion of the region. This group, now known as the Taíno,[1] inhabited what we know today as the Bahamas, most of Cuba, Jamaica, Haiti, the Dominican Republic, Puerto Rico, and several islands in the northern Lesser Antilles.

As a cultural group, traits unique to the Taíno included their own cosmology and associated religious practices and spiritual beliefs, their own customs and systems of social and political organization, their own forms of artistic expression, their own methods of farming and fishing, and more. In 1492 they were still expanding the reach of their influence and had been defending their eastern territories from invasions by a cultural group from the Lesser Antilles popularly known as the Caribs. The island of Puerto Rico, which the Taíno called Borikén, was one of the locations commonly targeted by Carib raiders. While this experience developed the inhabitants of Borikén into battle-experienced warriors, especially on the eastern end of the island, what they encountered in the military capacity of Spain was extraordinary.[2]

National Identity Born Out Of A Culture Of Resistance

The Taíno were the first people in the Americas to face the brutal system of European colonialism. They were also the first people in the Americas to develop an organized anti-colonial resistance movement. In Borikén this anti-colonial effort came to a head in 1511 when the cacique[3] Agüeybaná El Bravo[4] united several other caciques in the island, including the brothers Yaureibo and Cacimar of the neighboring island of Vieques, in a war against the Spaniards.[5] Lasting until 1518, with additional attacks from Taíno outposts continuing until 1529, the war forced countless Taínos into exile as the Spaniards destroyed their villages. Either choosing to assimilate into the emerging centers of colonial society or achieve some degree of separateness in the inner mountain regions, or something in between, remaining Taínos were able to maintain and pass on considerable parts of their culture and identity, easily found among contemporary Puerto Rican people.

After the slave trade of African people was brought to and amplified in the Caribbean, resistance to Spanish colonialism naturally continued. In his book based on official municipal records over the 78 years from 1795 to 1873, when slavery was abolished in Puerto Rico, Guillermo A. Baralt concluded "The number of known conspiracies to seize possession of the towns and of the island, plus incidents in which whites and particularly *mayordomos*[6] were murdered, is in excess of forty." Obviously, this does not include earlier periods or the many other acts and forms of resistance that took place or were used. As Baralt himself states, "given the covert and clandestine nature of these movements, the total is undoubtedly much higher. There were also hundreds of individual escapes that occurred on a daily basis, and which represented another form of rebellion against the institution of slavery."[7]

The Spanish government always gave preferential treatment to those Spaniards born in Spain over those born in the colonies of Spanish-descent, who came to be known as criollos. Eventually, this created yet another source of resistance to the colonial system as this growing class of criollos increasingly resented their situation. Worse for Spain, there were also residents born in Spain and from the land-owning and other privileged classes allying themselves with anti-colonial sentiment, even if only for moral or economic, rather than humanistic or revolutionary, reasons. Through the centuries, Taínos, Spaniards, Africans, indigenous people from other places in the Caribbean area brought in as slave labor, and people from other European countries, intermixed to wide-ranging degrees throughout the colonial territory. Over the generations, a defined national identity began to develop.

Boriken, the large island we know as Puerto Rico today, was initially given the name San Juan Bautista by Christopher Columbus in 1493, with the capital city being named Puerto Rico. Over time the names switched, the capital became known as San Juan, and the island became known as Puerto Rico. In a Spanish twist on the original indigenous name, residents also refer to the island as Borinquen. Both names for the island influenced the way native-born people identified themselves. For example, in the political writings connected to *El Grito de Lares*, the seminal 1868 revolt that sought to make Puerto Rico independent, both terms Puertorriqueños and Borinqueños were used.[8]

Of course, Puerto Rico also refers to an archipelago that has several smaller neighboring islands associated with its national territory, such as Vieques, Culebra, and Mona.

El Grito De Lares

El Grito de Lares, which began on September 23, 1868, is important for a few reasons. One way in which it has become historically significant is that it is used by many to mark the birth of the Puerto Rican nation, with the date it began, September 23, being considered its birthdate. The revolt, which also sought to abolish slavery, resulted in a declaration of independence but was defeated militarily by the colonial government the following day.

Tying the cultures of resistance that for centuries had defined those in opposition to the colonial regime—the Taíno who resisted the colonization of their land, the African people who resisted their enslavement, and the criollos who resisted their oppression—*El Grito de Lares* is significant as a major development of the national formation process. The idea of recognizing Puerto Rico as a nation was clearly receiving serious support.

Although 93% of the suspects identified by the colonial government as taking part in the revolt were native-born Puerto Ricans—all except 39 out of 551 suspects—there was also a noteworthy international aspect to *El Grito*. Besides having the participation of people born in Africa, some of the military leaders of the revolt were foreign-born.[9] Political statements put out by the revolutionaries made clear that foreign-born persons who participated in the struggle would be recognized as patriots.

Ultimately, the individuals appointed to serve as the heads of the government of the Republic of Puerto Rico, such as Francisco Ramírez Medina who was named its president, were all native-born Puerto Ricans. *El Grito*, centered in Lares and fought predominantly by native-born Puerto Ricans, saw the participation of a wide range of Puerto Rican society, with respect to race, class, age, town of residence, and more.[10]

Don Pedro's family lived through these events. His lineage that is tied to African-born people brought to Puerto Rico to work in the system of slavery would have, at the very least, been aware of the abolitionist focus of *El Grito*. While the revolt was militarily defeated, it did put pressure on the Spanish government to end slavery in Puerto Rico, which it eventually did less than five years later on March 22, 1873. His family, as well as Don Pedro himself, also lived through the transition from being a colony of the Spanish government to a colony of the United States government, a process that included the bombing of San Juan by U.S. Navy warships on May 12, 1898, and that was completed by the invasion of Guánica on July 25, 1898.

Chapter 2: The Birth Of Don Pedro

His Parents

Don Pedro's parents are Juliana Campos Campos and Alejandro Albizu y Romero. They have significantly different origins that converged in Ponce, Puerto Rico. Juliana was born in 1857 in Ponce's neighboring town of Juana Díaz, presumably into an enslaved status. Her mother, Ana María, was an enslaved woman of African descent that worked on a hacienda in that town owned by a man named Adolfo Campos.[11]

After Adolfo died, Juliana left the hacienda with her older sister Rosa and settled in a neighborhood[12] of Ponce that is said to have been established by formerly enslaved people after the abolition of slavery in 1873. Juliana's father was a man named Tomás that, according to accounts,[13] arrived in Puerto Rico from the U.S. South as an enslaved person.

Alejandro was born in 1844 Ponce where both his parents met after separately moving there in 1821 from Venezuela. Alejandro's father, Antonio Albizu Ordoñez, was of Basque origin and owned Hacienda Rita in Barrio Tercero where Alejandro served as *mayordomo*. According to the 1872 *Registro Central de Esclavos*,[14] twenty-two people were enslaved in Don Antonio's name, three of which were listed as being of direct African origin.[15]

Alejandro's mother, Rita Romero Molina, was the daughter of Francisco Romero, a two-time interim mayor of Ponce. Alejandro, who studied business administration in Baltimore, Maryland, is said to have considered joining the U.S. South during the Civil War but was dissuaded by his father. He eventually worked as an accountant and then as an administrator for the customs office in Ponce.[16]

Whatever the circumstances that brought about the meeting of Don Pedro's parents and his birth, it was not a simple matter. His father Alejandro was not only part of a landowning family that benefited from the work of enslaved people, but he was also married. His wife, with whom he had three children, was Cristina Antonsanti Romero. Consequently, when Juliana Campos gave birth to their child it was registered as 'illegitimate' with the name Pedro Campos and no mention of a father or second surname. It was not until the year 1914[17] that Don Pedro, in a short trip to Puerto Rico in the middle of his studies at Harvard University, went with his father to a Ponce law office and was legally recognized as his son, allowing him to take on the surname Albizu.

According to the racial categories common in Puerto Rico and much of the Caribbean, Don Pedro was born a mulatto.[18] Through his parents he inherited an ancestry composed of European and African elements, with his European ancestry coming from a unique cultural region known as the Basque Country that lies along the border between Spain and France. While his paternal side was European, landowning, and a benefactor of the institution of slavery, Don Pedro nevertheless spoke positively of his paternal family both in private and in public.

His Birthdate

There are two dates given as the birthdate of Pedro Albizu Campos— September 12, 1891 and June 29, 1893. The confusion around which date to use is frustrated further by the fact that, throughout his life, Don Pedro himself used both dates at different moments. Even worse, there were moments when Don Pedro used one date when discussing his birth date but gave an age that corresponded to being born on the other. Letters and statements by family and close associates don't provide any clarity either as they also wavered between the two dates.

The key to making sense of this double birthdate confusion lies in the belief of Don Pedro's mother that a person's spirit can be incorporated into the body of another person.[19] Having given birth to a child on the 12th of September 1891, Juliana Campos registered this child as Pedro Campos.[20] Not long after, this child passed away. Juliana then gave birth to another child on the 29th of June 1893, the Catholic feast day of San Pedro and San Pablo throughout Latin America.[21]

Due to her spiritual beliefs, coupled with the religious significance of the date, Juliana considered this child to have the spirit of her earlier-born son and maintained its name as Pedro. No birth records corresponding with the date of June 29, 1893 exist for this second child because Juliana did not go about the registration process. It was her belief that the child was a reincarnation of her earlier born—it was the same child.

As was said, Don Pedro used both dates at different times. For example, when he was admitted to Harvard University in 1913, the birthdate he wrote on his admissions papers was June 29, 1893. When he went with his father just a year later to be legally recognized by him, the date of birth he gave was September 12, 1891. What can be said from what is known is, in essence, the 'spiritual' birthdate of Pedro Albizu Campos is September 12, 1891, and his 'biological' birthdate is June 29, 1893.

Chapter 3: A Childhood In Ponce

Family And Neighborhood Environment

The neighborhood in which Don Pedro was born, Barrio Machuelo Abajo, was established not far from the Río Bucaná. As a child, like many others in the community, Don Pedro used the river to bathe. His home was one among many homes built of wood with straw thatched roofs. The entire neighborhood was without electricity. When Don Pedro reminisced about his youth during a February 1948 speech, he highlighted the sense of community, saying, "all of the children of Puerto Rico encountered in every Puerto Rican woman a mother, and in every Puerto Rican man a father."[22]

Don Pedro's mother Juliana was challenged with mental health issues and was known to wander the street all day talking to herself. On one occasion she burned garbage inside of their home, causing a fire that damaged its interior. On another occasion she took Don Pedro and a second child under her arms to the river in an attempt to drown herself with them, but her sister Rosa intervened. Juliana eventually did die of drowning on October 4, 1895, leaving Don Pedro orphaned under the care of Rosa. In the 1910 Census, Don Pedro was listed in Rosa's household as her son.[23]

The oral history given by Ruth Reynolds to the Center for Puerto Rican Studies provides several insights[24] into Don Pedro's childhood. His relationship with his aunt Rosa, for example, appears to have been rocky at times, with a young Don Pedro feeling she could be overly strict.

Apparently, there was a period when he regularly ran away from her home. When he did this it is said he usually ended up spending time with a 100+ year old black man he had befriended and who impressed upon the young Don Pedro gentlemanly, yet gendered ideas regarding the treatment of women. When this man died Don Pedro was devastated, both because of his death and because he no longer had a place to run away to.

Childhood Activities

As a child Don Pedro is said to have been inclined towards sports and physical activity. He played baseball and took up the habit of jogging. Having good aim with a slingshot, accounts say that Don Pedro killed a few birds but then refused to do so anymore. In an interesting parallel to a common sport in Basque Country where his paternal family is from, Don Pedro is also said to have regularly lifted the heavy, rounded stones he found along the Río Bucaná. One account also says Don Pedro liked to train animals and was able to train goats to perform tricks.

Growing up with his aunt Rosa, weekly visits to the local church for Sunday Catholic Mass became a consistent part of his childhood. One story related by the late Puerto Rican nationalist Isabel Rosado explains how Don Pedro always took off his shoes for the long walk to church as they were not comfortable for traveling such a long distance. At church he noticed people looking in his and his aunt's direction and assumed it was because of his aunt's hat. He later realized that they were paying attention to him because he was in the church barefoot, his shoes tied around his neck and hanging down both sides of his body.

According to Ruth Reynolds, Don Pedro remembered a time when he was about 12 years old and was causing his family much difficulty due to his behavior. His father Alejandro apparently hired a young man named Simón to keep him company. During the time they spent together Simón taught Don Pedro to dive and swim better, as well as other things. It was around this time that Don Pedro remembers being beaten by his aunt Rosa and then running away from home, hiding in trees and eating fruit for 2-3 days until he turned himself in to his friends. His father once again stepped in and told Rosa that if she ever used corporal punishment again, he would take Don Pedro away from her.[25]

Clearly, Don Pedro had some relationship during his childhood with his father even before he was legally recognized by him in 1914. Don Pedro told Ruth Reynolds that his father visited him often as a child. Reynolds was also told by Don Pedro's wife that he once lived with a paternal aunt in Ponce for a period. In his research on Don Pedro as a university student, scholar Anthony De Jesús found that, on his application to Harvard, Don Pedro wrote of having traveled to Brazil, Cuba, Santo Domingo, Venezuela, and "other West Indies" between 1907 and 1909.[26] Presumably, this traveling was done with his father (see table on next page).

Location	Date(s)
Cuba	1907 (4 months)
Santo Domingo	1908 (2 months)
Brazil	1909 (1 month)
Venezuela	Unknown
"Other West Indies"	Unknown

Don Pedro's Travels From 1907-1909

Chapter 4: Early Success In School

Choosing To Attend School

Attending school at the time that Don Pedro was born apparently was not a given for him. Under his aunt Rosa's care, he was not immediately enrolled in school when he was of school age. In her biography on Don Pedro, historian Marisa Rosado states that he entered school at the age of 12 and at the insistence of his friends. An account by Ruth Reynolds provides a slightly different perspective.

According to Reynolds, one day Don Pedro took notice of a group of kids looking "all cleaned up" in their attire and asked them where they were going. When they responded that they were going to school they also inquired about his going to school. In this story, it was at that point that Don Pedro told his aunt Rosa that he wanted to go, to which she replied, "change your clothes."[27]

Rosado points to a school in Ponce headed by a woman named Doña Rosa Percy as where Don Pedro first began his studies. However long he stayed there, he ultimately found himself at the McKinley Agricultural School, where instruction was led by a single North American teacher named Mr. Cooper. Don Pedro was remembered as being a good student, taking a lot of notes in class, and studying at night using an oil lamp. He was also remembered for providing support to other students as needed.

Don Pedro completed the first eight grades in the four years between 1905 and 1909. An exceptional student committed to learning, Don Pedro was documented in the 1910 Census as being able to speak English, a skill probably developed by his North American teacher Mr. Cooper.

Building A Reputation At Ponce High School

Academically, the coursework at Ponce High School focused on the general subjects we are familiar with today. On his cumulative transcript, Don Pedro was documented as having taken four years of English; three years of Latin; two years of History, Spanish, and French; and one year of Algebra, Physics, Geometry, and Zoology. Besides an 88 received in the third quarter of his first year in French, all his grades were in the 90s.

At Ponce High School, Don Pedro's opportunity to further his education was coupled with opportunities to gain recognition outside of his school. He set himself apart as a captivating public speaker and debater, one time serving as the school's debate team captain for a contest held in English. In 1910 he was chosen to represent his school in a notable public speaking contest in Mayagüez. The contest was presided over by none other than José De Diego, a statesman, journalist, poet, and an important Puerto Rican historical figure that became known as the "father of the Puerto Rican independence movement." Not only did Don Pedro win the contest, but De Diego personally awarded him the prize and was so impressed that he later played a role in securing Don Pedro a scholarship to attend college.

While known for having a great sense of humor, Don Pedro's greatest reputation was as an intellectual, a skilled speaker, and a student leader. Dr. José Padín, who was a local school superintendent and then public schools commissioner in the years Don Pedro was in high school, said in a 1950 interview with the *Boston Globe* that he was a "child prodigy" and "oratorical spellbinder." Don Pedro was also developing as a writer during this time. Following the death of a classmate named Mercedes Castaing in 1911, he was published in the *Puerto Rico Eagle* newspaper. The article, written in English at 18 years old, is an eloquent, heartfelt, and poetic display of emotion, spiritual contemplation, and reverence for the dead.[28]

Graduating With Honors

Don Pedro graduated from Ponce High School in 1912 with distinguished honors. Some accounts say that Don Pedro, with a cumulative average of 95.93, graduated as the valedictorian of his class, while another account places him as the salutatorian. What is without question is that the young 'prodigy' made a strong reputation for himself.

The impression Don Pedro made on José De Diego worked to his favor in July 1912 when De Diego, at the time the president of the Puerto Rico House of Delegates, quickly approved a recommendation sent to him by the secretary of the Municipal Council of Ponce to grant Don Pedro a scholarship to attend college. Becoming more than a recommendation, Don Pedro eventually did receive this scholarship.

In August 1912 he was considered for another scholarship by the Masonic Lodge "Aurora" No. 7 of Ponce. This consideration was recommended by E. N. Gerrish, the principal of Ponce High School, and Charles H. Terry, the superintendent of schools in Ponce. Don Pedro also received this scholarship. According to the account given by Ruth Reynolds, it was Gerrish, as an alumnus of the University of Vermont, who also helped to fill out most of the paperwork that resulted in Don Pedro being admitted as a student there for September 1912.[29]

Notes To Chapters 1 - 4

[1] The word Taíno has been used as an umbrella term by anthropologists for this regional indigenous cultural group. In truth, the people identified themselves with the land. For example, the natives of the large island of Puerto Rico called both their land and themselves Borikén.

[2] Stevens-Arroyo, *Cave of the Jagua*; Wilson, *Archaeology of the Caribbean*; Rouse, *The Tainos*.

[3] Indigenous title for a local or regional leader.

[4] He was the brother of Agüeybaná, the leader of all other caciques of Puerto Rico that welcomed Ponce de León.

[5] Badillo. *Agüeybaná El Bravo*.

[6] The heads of large estates.

[7] Baralt, *Slave Revolts In Puerto Rico*.

[8] *Puertorriqueños* was used in the 10 Commandments of Free Men written by Ramón Emeterio Betances, the leader of El Grito considered the father of the Puerto Rican nation; *Borinqueños* was used in La Borinqueña, a song written by Lola Rodríguez de Tió in support of the independence movement that became the national anthem of Puerto Rico.

[9] Ex. Manuel Rojas, Commander of the Liberation Army, was born in Venezuela; Matías Brugman was born in New Orleans, Louisiana of Dutch ancestry; Francisco Dorval Beauchamp Sterling was born in Haiti of French ancestry.

[10] Jiménez de Wagenheim, *El Grito De Lares*.

[11] Rosado, *Las Llamas de la Aurora*.

[12] It is often said that they lived in Barrio Tenerías. Technically, and according to census records, the barrio they lived in was Machuelo Abajo, within which Tenerías was a sector.

[13] Ruth Reynolds, a North American pacifist activist that befriended Don Pedro, is one source. For more on Reynolds, see Chapter 24.

[14] 'Slave Schedules' in English, this record contains information (Name, Age, Country of origin, Parents' names, Marital status, etc.) for all persons in Puerto Rico classified as slaves in that year.

[15] Ancestry.com, *Puerto Rico, Registro Central de Esclavos, 1872*.

[16] Center for Puerto Rican Studies Library and Archives, *Oral History, The Ruth M. Reynolds Papers*.

[17] According to a note written on the original 1891 birth record, this legal recognition of Don Pedro as Alejandro's son took place on September 10, 1914.

[18] Ancestry.com, *1910 United States Federal Census*.

[19] This understanding is part of the tradition of espiritismo, a belief system and practice built on the idea that a spirit realm not only exists but is an integral part of physical reality that we can also interact with.

[20] Ancestry.com, *Puerto Rico, Civil Registrations, 1885-2001*.

[21] whoisalbizu, *Interview with José Enrique Ayoroa Santaliz*.

[22] Rosado, *Las Llamas de la Aurora*.

[23] Ancestry.com, *1910 United States Federal Census*.

[24] After Reynolds befriended Don Pedro in 1943 New York City she spent a lot of time and was able to interact with him on a very frequent basis.

[25] Center for Puerto Rican Studies Library and Archives, *Oral History, The Ruth M. Reynolds Papers*.

[26] De Jesús, *I have endeavored*.

[27] Center for Puerto Rican Studies Library and Archives, *Oral History, The Ruth M. Reynolds Papers*.

[28] Center for Puerto Rican Studies Library and Archives, *Historical Journals and Periodicals*.

[29] Rosado, *Las Llamas de la Aurora*.

Second Period — University Experience

Chapter 5: Studies In New England

Academics In The University Of Vermont And Harvard

When Don Pedro entered the University of Vermont in 1912 for its fall semester his major was agricultural engineering. Becoming known among students for wearing a black fedora hat, Don Pedro also became known among teachers and faculty for his unmistakable intellect. This recognition among teachers and faculty resulted in his being recommended and pushed to attend Harvard University, which he did starting the following fall semester of 1913. Don Pedro eventually became the first Puerto Rican to graduate from Harvard.

At Harvard Don Pedro's interest in engineering continued but would now focus on chemical engineering. In addition to coursework related to chemistry, he also took classes on government, economics, and languages. Except for his second year, during which he suffered from an illness that affected his eyes and ability to study for several weeks, Don Pedro fared well in his coursework. Resilient and persistent, in June 1916 he graduated with a degree in chemical engineering in addition to a Bachelor of Arts degree in Philosophy and Letters. In good standing as a student, Don Pedro was accepted into Harvard Law School, beginning classes that following September of 1916.

His decision to study law would go on to have a significant impact on his development. Studying law from several perspectives, including international law, he began to further develop his ideology regarding the situation of Puerto Rico.[1] Despite some significant obstacles, Don Pedro eventually completed all course requirements and earned his Doctor of Law degree, at the time called a Bachelor of Laws (LL.B.). In a testament to his incredible capacity to learn, he also had a command of eight languages: his native Spanish, English, Portuguese, French, Italian, German, Latin, and Greek. During these years, Don Pedro also gained considerable attention on campus as a student leader.

Participating In Organizations And Activism

Beyond his academic accomplishments, Don Pedro was also an activist and a member of several student and other organizations, many times in a leadership position. Among these organizations are the American Chemical Society, the Boylston Chemical Club, the Cosmopolitan Club, the International Polity Club, the League to Enforce Peace, the Speakers Club, and the St. Paul's Catholic Club. Don Pedro is also credited as a founder of the Harvard chapter of the Knights of Columbus, an organization closely associated with the Catholic Church.[2]

Don Pedro began his public activism as soon as he arrived at the University of Vermont. During his one year there he is known to have spoken on the education of women in Latin America in a student forum and, on another occasion in a public discussion, against U.S. intervention in Mexico. At Harvard he is known to have given lectures on the situation in Puerto Rico at the College Street Club, the assimilation of immigrants at the American Society of Colonial Families, the Monroe Doctrine at the Socialist Club of Boston, and the conditions of black people in Latin America at the Public Opinion Club.

Recognized and respected by his peers as an intelligent student leader and engaging speaker, Don Pedro was elected president for both the Cosmopolitan Club and League to Enforce Peace. For most of his Harvard years Don Pedro was selected to welcome foreign students and visitors from other countries, sometimes serving as a translator. When the Indian poet and first non-European to win the Nobel Prize in Literature,

Rabindranath Tagore, visited Harvard, Don Pedro was selected by his law student peers to lead the reception ceremony. Later, when the Irish patriot Éamon de Valera visited Harvard for a conference, Don Pedro was again selected to serve as one of the lead hosts.

Financial Struggles And Racial Discrimination

In his article on Don Pedro's university studies, scholar Anthony De Jesús highlights his financial situation.[3] Acknowledging that while he did receive a Price Greenleaf scholarship awarded to low-income students, Don Pedro still had to cover a significant amount of tuition and living expenses on his own. Thus, on top of all the time and energy devoted to his studies and as a leader and activist in school and local organizations, Don Pedro also had to work. He tutored classmates in Spanish, French, and Chemistry; he taught Spanish as a professor at two local schools; he wrote for the Christian Science Monitor and two Puerto Rican newspapers; and, at one point, due an inability to find anything else, he cut grass.

Besides financial struggles, Don Pedro also faced racial discrimination, most notably, as highlighted in the article by De Jesús, by his own teachers. One teacher commented that his manner was pleasant and his coursework noteworthy, "especially when considering that he is a Porto Rican." Another teacher, out of prejudice and to prevent him from securing his place as valedictorian of his graduating class, prevented Don Pedro from taking the final exams for two required law courses. Returning to Puerto Rico in 1921, Don Pedro was forced to correspond with the university and obtain permission to have the exams administered in Puerto Rico.

After back-and-forth correspondence from Puerto Rico to Harvard, Don Pedro took his remaining final exams in June 1922 and was finally awarded his diploma in the beginning of 1923. He was sworn in as an official lawyer in Puerto Rico in the beginning of 1924.[4] De Jesús draws a parallel with Puerto Rican and Latino/a students of today by highlighting Don Pedro's academic and personal challenges related to his health, his financial struggles, and his subjection to racial discrimination. De Jesús, as others have before him, also points out the clear presence of key influences that later found expression in Don Pedro's leadership of Puerto Rico's independence movement, namely Catholicism and the Indian and Irish struggles for national independence.

Chapter 6: Solidarity And Spirituality

Support Of Indian And Irish Independence

While attending Harvard University, Don Pedro is known for engaging with events and issues relating to Latin America and countries throughout the world, and to have been greatly influenced by the revolutionary movements existing at the time in India and Ireland. Regarding the movement for Indian independence from British rule, as previously mentioned, Don Pedro was selected to represent Harvard in the welcome reception for the visiting Indian poet Rabindranath Tagore. At this reception Don Pedro spoke following Tagore's welcoming speech and commented on his definition of nationalism.[5]

Don Pedro's views on the forms of struggle being adopted in India, which included Mohandas Gandhi's non-violence, are said to have been more aligned with those elements that favored armed struggle, with the Indian nationalist Bal Gangadhar Tilak being the most cited example.

While this may be true, it should also be made clear that he was also able to articulate a profound appreciation for aspects of the non-violent forms of struggle. This was made most explicit when, in a 1948 article[6] just days after the passing of Gandhi, he wrote the following:

> *"The whole of India was made to embrace the recovery of its national will and accept non-cooperation with the foreign despotism that subjugated it, as the effective force to destroy it... Gandhi for the whole world represents the infinite power of the spirit. Already almost a skeleton... The Mahatma taught us that Power is within us. And that freedom must be first in the soul and it will be invincible; it will prevail over all despotisms."*

The revolutionary movement of the Irish people in their own struggle against British colonial rule would be an even greater influence. In this movement Don Pedro saw elements comparable to the situation of Puerto Rico that he emphasized in his leadership years later: a predominantly Catholic island nation with its own language, history, and culture facing a large, predominantly Protestant, English-speaking empire. As a student leader Don Pedro had the opportunity to personally meet Éamon De Valera, a prominent Irish revolutionary leader, during a 1919 visit to Harvard during a conference that Don Pedro also provided remarks in.

Following the bloody 1916 Easter Rebellion in Ireland, Don Pedro's strong, unwavering support of full Irish independence was at odds with the predominantly conservative leanings of Harvard students and faculty. Undeterred by this climate, Don Pedro helped organize student councils in support of Irish independence at Harvard, Boston Technical College, and Boston College. He organized conferences, debates, and demonstrations in support of the Irish cause and collected donations outside factories and in Irish communities to give directly to it.[7]

Don Pedro's committed support of Irish independence was so genuine and clear that, on one occasion in front of an audience of 1,400 students, faculty, and foreign diplomats gathered to debate the topic, he delivered a speech resulting in a standing ovation. This ovation was interrupted by a member of the British Parliament on diplomatic leave compelled to say, "I am a British nobleman, so there is no need to inquire my opinion on the Irish question. But gentlemen I would not be a Britisher, I would not be a nobleman, if I failed to admit that Mr. Campos has just delivered the most complete, the most brilliant speech on this matter, that I have ever heard."

Thanks to his reputation as an unyielding supporter of their cause, before the Constitution of the Irish Free State was adopted in 1922 Don Pedro was consulted while it was being drafted. The influence of the Irish revolutionary struggle on his political thinking cannot be overstated. In fact, in an interview regarding her book *Ireland and Puerto Rico: The Untold Story*, author Aoife Rivera Serrano stated that Don Pedro's struggle was "entirely modeled on the Irish struggle against Britain."[8] The book *Nosotros Solos: Pedro Albizu Campos y el Nacionalismo Irlandés* by Juan Angel Silén is devoted entirely to examining this connection.

Committing To A Spiritual Path

In addition to an active identification with Ireland's revolutionary struggle, another critical influence on Don Pedro's political development was his personal commitment to Catholicism.[9] Providing details about his decision to convert, the Puerto Rican poet and independence activist Juan Antonio Corretjer points to a priest named Father Ryan as guiding Don Pedro to make communion, and another priest named Father Luis Rodes, an astronomer of Catalonian descent, as impressing upon Don Pedro the unity of science with faith.[10] The fact that there was a large Irish community in Boston observant of the religion also meant that Don Pedro would have come into contact with many devout Catholics during his work in support of Ireland's independence.

Though an active member of St. Paul's Catholic Club and a founder of Harvard's Knights of Columbus, it is clear that Don Pedro adopted Catholicism for intellectual reasons rather than out of a purely religious experience. The reading of one specific text from 1842, *El Protestantismo Comparado con el Catolicismo* by the Spanish-born Jaime Balmes, is cited as a probable factor in the evolution of Don Pedro's thinking. In this text Balmes argues, among other things, that Catholic and Spanish values are superior to Protestant and Northern European values in their respect of local cultures, customs, and languages. Additionally, Balmes quotes Irish patriots to emphasize his point regarding the failure of Protestants to secure Ireland's freedom despite their claims of bringing Enlightenment and democracy.

In his essay on Don Pedro's 'Catholic worldview,' scholar Anthony M. Stevens-Arroyo points to three factors as serving to intensify his affinity with Balmes' ideas.[11] First, he highlights the influence on Don Pedro of the militant organizing and martyrdom of the Irish patriot James Connolly, a leader in the 1916 Easter Rebellion. Second, he highlights Don Pedro's membership in the Knights of Columbus and that organization's active use of Catholicism in support of patriotic ideals. Third, he highlights the prominent discussion of international law as it relates to independence for oppressed nationalities at the Versailles Peace Conference during the formation of the League of Nations after World War 1.

In another analysis on the approach to his faith, Don Pedro's daughter Cristina Meneses Albizu-Campos suggested that his Christian spirituality was unifying and singularly oriented to the project of national liberation for Puerto Rico. Pointing out the various creeds of the people that took part in the nationalist movement under his leadership—"Catholics, Protestants, *Espiritistas*, Masons, Atheists, Agnostics"—she highlights the Catholic sense of service and sacrifice for others that defined Don Pedro's political work. Without a doubt, it is this Catholic/religious sense of "duty to help others take the path of humanity," as she described it, that profoundly influenced Don Pedro in Harvard.[12]

Chapter 7: R.O.T.C. Training At Harvard

Deciding To Receive Military Training During WW1

When the First World War began on July 28, 1914, Don Pedro had recently finished his first year at Harvard. An active participant in student affairs on campus, he was exposed to many debates and discussions on the war held by student organizations, many of which included the participation of faculty. The three points of view generally debated and discussed were: support for U.S. President Woodrow Wilson's initial stance of 'isolationism' and the avoidance of all involvement in the war; support for the Allied Powers; and support for the Central Powers.

On November 10, 1915, a university forum was convened at Harvard and a debate was held on whether the U.S. should provide the Allied Forces moral and economic support.[13] A vote was taken and 47 said no to providing support, with 21 saying yes to providing support. By this time, however, a movement for 'preparedness' was already gaining momentum throughout the U.S. with the support of President Wilson who was changing from his earlier isolationist stance. On November 30 the *Harvard Crimson* paper announced a resolution by the student council, inspired by this preparedness movement, to organize a company of students to receive instruction in military science.[14] In this dynamic and polemical environment, Don Pedro decided to pursue military training.

As far as the specific views Don Pedro held, on one undated occasion known to be before the U.S. officially entered the war on April 6, 1917, he is known to have argued the side of the Allied Powers during a public discussion hosted by the Diplomatic Club. He received a large ovation and, a few days later, a special invitation by the club to become a member. On April 14, eight days after the U.S. entered the war, the *Harvard Crimson* published an article he authored titled "Porto Rico and the War."[15] In this article Don Pedro wrote about Puerto Ricans welcoming the U.S. flag in 1898 as a symbol originally conceived to represent "democracy and justice." He also said, about the war, "there is no division among us, we detest German tyranny and arrogance, and we will give good account of ourselves in actual voluntary military co-operation with the United States."

The company of students organized at Harvard became known as the Harvard Regiment and was officially approved by the university president on February 10, 1916.[16] Following the passing by Congress of the National Defense Act of 1916 on June 3rd, the university eventually reorganized it into the Harvard Reserve Officers Training Corps program, one of the first R.O.T.C. programs created in the U.S. While his membership in the Harvard Regiment is not clear, we do know that it is the R.O.T.C. program that Don Pedro was a part of. That program immediately began instruction but was not officially recognized by the government until February 1917.[17]

The R.O.T.C. Training That Don Pedro Received

The commander of Harvard's military program, appointed by the U.S. War Department, was Captain Constant Cordier. In his first speech to the Harvard Regiment on January 4, 1916, he detailed the approach he was taking, stating that the focus would be on the infantry training that all branches of the military are based on.[18]

When the R.O.T.C. program was initiated that Fall, it became apparent that the number of officers and non-commissioned officers running the program was not sufficient. Nevertheless, in that time when the Harvard R.O.T.C. program was under his command, Captain Cordier and his team managed to provide the course 'Military Science and Tactics 1' in addition to "close and open order drill, gallery practice, and bayonet instruction."

The need for more personnel was finally addressed in April 1917. Using the recent U.S. declaration of war as leverage, the president of Harvard was able to get approval from the U.S. War Department and French government to host disabled and/or retired French officers willing to assist with the R.O.T.C. program's instruction. The head of this group would be Lieutenant Colonel Paul Azan. According to an article in the *Harvard Crimson*, this group provided lectures on "various important phases of modern warfare as the grenade, the automatic rifle, the machine gun, field fortifications, trench routine, principles of infantry in modern combat, and the role of the high command."

At the start of June, three battalions of cadets[19] took turns camping for a week on a range where they were trained in firing rifles, surviving in the field, and more. Following this event, now the end of the academic year, Captain Cordier was given military orders away from Harvard, at which point Captain James Shannon, who had been with the program from its beginning though mostly tending to office work, was named the new R.O.T.C. commander.

Cadets continued to be instructed in infantry tactics, map sketching, and general military science, and began preparation for three weeks of field training at Camp Barre. During these three weeks, from July 23 to August 11, cadets lived in shelter tents and conducted training maneuvers during both the day and night. This served as the culmination of that first Harvard R.O.T.C. class, of which Don Pedro was a part.[20]

It is worth taking a moment, as others writing about Don Pedro's development during this period have, to put into perspective all the qualities and influences present at this point. He has been acknowledged as gifted with a genius-level intelligence and talent for public speaking. He has been increasingly active as a vocal supporter and organizer in favor of anti-colonial revolutionary struggles. He converted to Catholicism and adopted a spiritual approach to dignity and sacrifice in service of others. He entered law school at a time when international law was at the global forefront. He volunteered to receive military training as a cadet in Harvard's R.O.T.C. program. All of these are significant elements recognized as key factors in Don Pedro's form and style of leadership years later in Puerto Rico. That they are all present within this one period at Harvard is noteworthy and underlines the formative experience that his time at Harvard was.[21]

Chapter 8: Lieutenant Campos

Commissioning As An Infantry Officer In Puerto Rico

Despite the U.S. War Department's authorization of Harvard's R.O.T.C. program, and the acknowledgment of its success by government officials including generals and the secretary of war, none of the 1,885 members that received instruction in that first class were given a commission as officers at graduation. Instead, they were given a recommendation for commission. In Don Pedro's case, he was recommended for commission as a first lieutenant.[22]

In September 1917, one month after completing the Harvard R.O.T.C. program, Don Pedro presented himself before General Frank McIntyre of the Bureau of Insular Affairs to express his desire to fight in World War 1. Requesting to serve in an infantry regiment specifically based in Puerto Rico, Don Pedro's request was denied, and the War Department advised him to continue his law studies and await further instructions. After the 1917-1918 school year, during which time he never heard back from the War Department, Don Pedro renewed his efforts to join the war, this time with success. As soon as he finished his Spring semester exams, he made his way to New York City and boarded the SS Coamo traveling to San Juan from May 4 to May 9.

On July 10, 1918, Don Pedro signed enlistment papers in Ponce as a private for a length of service defined as "for duration of War." He then underwent additional training as part of D Company in the Third Officers Training Camp.[23] On November 6, of the 278 men who enlisted into the training camp, 253 graduated and received a commission as a second lieutenant. Another 23, including Don Pedro, graduated and received a commission as a first lieutenant. All were to serve as infantry officers. Only eight of the second lieutenant graduates were classified as "colored." Among first lieutenant graduates, only Don Pedro was classified as "colored."[24]

As a commissioned officer Don Pedro seems to have had two main responsibilities during his time serving in the U.S. Army in Puerto Rico: training with the 375th Infantry Regiment and organizing a company of "Home Guards." The 375th Infantry Regiment was one of the Army's segregated all-black units whose sole purpose was to train and await possible orders for deployment to the overseas frontlines of the war. The Home Guard was an all-volunteer unit of those not able to serve in an active military capacity due to their age or condition but who could serve as a defense force in Puerto Rico in the event those in the active military were deployed. Don Pedro led this Home Guard effort in Ponce where some 200 volunteers were militarily trained on the local beaches.[25]

Missing Out On A Deployment To Europe

The 375th Infantry Regiment trained under the impression they could be deployed at any moment, Don Pedro himself even saying once that their transports were prepared, and they were ready to go. Nevertheless, the war came to an end before the regiment was activated. Stating he was one of five officers to "wind up the affairs of the regiment," Don Pedro was soon discharged from the service, in March 1919. The end of the war also brought about the dissolution of the Home Guards. Offered a follow-on commission as a first lieutenant in a Reserve unit, Don Pedro refused.

A few months before, on January 25, there was an article in the *Harvard Crimson* announcing a fundraising event taking place to help cover the expenses of sending a student delegate to the Paris Peace Conference in Europe.[26] In the article Don Pedro was named as the club's nominee. Seemingly unaware of this nomination until receiving a cablegram in April from the president of Harvard's Cosmopolitan Club, Don Pedro was presented with the challenge of traveling out of Puerto Rico with little planning time, during a period when all ships were being dedicated to the war effort.

Using his status as an honorably discharged Army officer, Don Pedro was able to leave Puerto Rico on a warship and begin his way to Harvard to report for his mission. Having to first travel through the U.S. South, beginning in Galveston, Texas, the trip had a deep impact on Don Pedro.[27] He witnessed the violent, humiliating racism of the U.S. South first-hand. Unfortunately, by the time Don Pedro arrived at Harvard, the rest of the student delegation had already left. He stayed behind and prepared for the 1919-20 school year.

The Need For Military Training For Puerto Ricans

In his April 14, 1917 article in the *Harvard Crimson*, Don Pedro wrote specifically about Puerto Ricans entering World War 1 in order to help defend the cause of the United States and the Allied Powers. In a 1926 interview published in *Los Quijotes*, a magazine in Puerto Rico, he shared his thoughts on the need for Puerto Ricans to receive military training in general, saying:

> *"[O]ur participation in the European War would have been of great benefit to the people of Puerto Rico. The military organization of a people is necessary for its defense and such is only achieved with the painful sacrifices that a war imposes."*

Juan Antonio Corretjer claimed that Don Pedro made an aborted attempt to organize an insurrectionist faction within the company of Home Guards he established in Ponce. After inviting a friend to take part in this effort, Don Pedro was responded to with laughter. When his friend realized Don Pedro was serious, he advised him to never share the idea again, as anybody else would betray and report him. Corretjer explained that Don Pedro believed Puerto Ricans returning from WW1 as combat veterans could serve as the core of "an independence movement capable of reorganizing the country's will against the Yankees."[28]

In his 1926 *Los Quijotes* interview, Don Pedro addressed why he had denied, at the end of WW1, a commission as first lieutenant in a Reserve unit. Saying that Puerto Ricans should not form part of the military organizations of the United States, he specifically rejected the idea of developing a "*Cipayo* Army of Puerto Rico." The term was used by Don Pedro in reference to the professional infantry soldiers native to India that were recruited and employed to serve the British and French East India Companies. Don Pedro was clear in his belief in the need for Puerto Ricans to organize a military capacity in their homeland—he further believed such should be enthusiastically focused on defending Puerto Rico's own interests.

School/Institution	Months/Years	Degree(s)/Notes
Primary School (Juana Díaz/Ponce)	1905 - 1909	
Ponce High School	Sep 1909 - 1912	Class President
University of Vermont	Sep 25, 1912 - 1913	Attended on scholarship
Harvard University	Sep 1913 - 1916	Philosophy & Letters (A.B); Chemistry
Harvard Law	Sep 25, 1916 - May 1918	Paused studies for military service in PR
Harvard R.O.T.C.	1916 - 1917	First Harvard R.O.T.C. class
Third Officers' Training Camp (PR)	Jul - Nov 1918	Commissioned as First Lieutenant
U.S. Army, 375th Infantry Regiment (PR)	Nov 1918 - Mar 1919	Served as First Lieutenant; Organized Home Guard
Harvard Law	Sep 27, 1919 - Jun 23, 1921	Law Degree (Awarded 1923)

Don Pedro's Academic And Military Record

Notes To Chapters 5 - 8

[1] Delgado Cintrón, *El Derecho En Pedro Albizu Campos*.

[2] Laura de Albizu Campos, *Albizu Campos y la Independencia de Puerto Rico*.

[3] De Jesús, *I have endeavored*.

[4] Rosado, *Las Llamas de la Aurora*.

[5] Rosado, *Las Llamas de la Aurora*.

[6] Albizu-Campos Meneses and Fr. Rodríguez León, eds., *Escritos*.

[7] Denis, *War Against All Puerto Ricans*.

[8] PR Web, *Ireland and Puerto Rico*.

[9] Sánchez Huertas, *Algunas Ideas Tentativas*.

[10] Corretjer, *Albizu Campos and the Ponce Massacre*.

[11] Stevens-Arroyo, *The Catholic Worldview in the Political Philosophy of Pedro Albizu Campos*.

[12] Meneses Albizu-Campos, *La Espiritualidad de Pedro Albizu Campos*.

[13] The Harvard Crimson, *Forum Decided Against Giving Aid To Allies*.

[14] The Harvard Crimson, *Voluntary Military Drill*.

[15] Albizu Campos, *Porto Rico and the War*.

[16] The Harvard Crimson, *University Regiment Officially Approved*.

[17] The Harvard Crimson, *Training Corps Is Officially Established*.

[18] The Harvard Crimson, *Regiment Commander Gave Detailed Plans*.

[19] College students that are members of an R.O.T.C. program are known as cadets.

[20] The Harvard Crimson, *R.O.T.C. Training Completed Successfully At Barre*. The Harvard Graduates' Magazine Association, *The Harvard Graduates' Magazine, Volume XXV. 1916-1917*.

[21] Rosado, *Las Llamas de la Aurora*.

[22] The Harvard Crimson, *R.O.T.C. Training Completed Successfully At Barre*.

[23] Established three weeks prior on June 21 at Camp Las Casas, it trained Puerto Ricans, primarily those who could classify as white, to become infantry officers.

[24] Negroni, *Historia Militar de Puerto Rico*.

[25] Franqui-Rivera, *The Porto Rican Division*.

---

[26] The Harvard Crimson, *Cosmopolitan Club Plans for "International Night"* Feb. 21.

[27] Laura de Albizu Campos, *Albizu Campos y la Independencia de Puerto Rico.*

[28] Rosado, *Las Llamas de la Aurora.*

Third Period — Early Professional Life

Chapter 9: Adult Life In Puerto Rico

Living A Life With Dignity

When Don Pedro left Puerto Rico in 1912 for his university studies, he was a 19-year-old with incredible potential. When Don Pedro returned to Puerto Rico permanently in 1921, he was a full-fledged 28-year-old young adult that had gone through a series of deeply formative experiences over the course of nine years. Now his responsibility was to find a way to make a living in his homeland.

After graduating from Harvard Law School, several job offers were extended to Don Pedro: as an assistant in the U.S. Supreme Court, a U.S. diplomat to Mexico, and an executive position in a U.S. corporation. Upon returning to Puerto Rico, he was also offered a position as a judge in the town of Yauco. For reasons never directly addressed in public, he turned down all the jobs offered to him and decided instead to start a law practice in Ponce. Of course, the reason he refused these jobs was his decision to serve the people of Puerto Rico, a commitment that also meant avoiding collaboration with the colonial regime.[1]

Essentially practicing poverty law, Don Pedro's clients were by and large the working-class poor who could only afford to pay for his services in chickens, vegetables, and other items in their possession. On occasion, a simple 'thank you' was Don Pedro's only form of compensation.

In his law practice Don Pedro only took on civil cases, except for divorce cases due to his embrace of Catholicism. He refused to take on criminal cases no matter how petty or potentially lucrative. When asked to take on a case that could result in a ten-thousand-dollar settlement, half going to Don Pedro, he refused and stated that he does not devote his services to such cases. The point he made was that, instead of being given five thousand dollars for his services, he was being used by the perpetrator to gain five thousand dollars for themselves. Don Pedro's insistence on having a dignified law practice based on the principle of being in service to the poor and oppressed of society meant that he had few clients and even less in the way of earnings.

In her biography on Don Pedro, author Marisa Rosado wrote, "the great profession of Albizu is that of Patriot." The secretary for Don Pedro's law practice, Víctor Bonó Rodríguez, said that most of his time during this period was spent giving lectures. Don Pedro made a routine of speaking every Sunday on a podium in Ponce's town square to anyone interested in hearing his analysis of current events, history, local/national affairs, and more. It was in these years following his permanent return to Puerto Rico that Don Pedro earned the title and nickname *El Maestro*, the teacher.[2] During this time, he was also invited to take part in conferences and other events in Ponce as well as neighboring towns, including one in his alma mater of Ponce High School.

The Beginnings Of Married Life

In this period, Don Pedro is building both a law practice and a family. Towards the end of his time at Harvard, in December 1920, Don Pedro met and very quickly established a serious relationship with Laura Emilia Meneses del Carpio,[3] a Peruvian and the first Latina accepted into Radcliffe College, the all-female section of Harvard. Doña Laura traveled to Ponce in July 1922 and, on the 10th of that month, exchanged vows with Don Pedro in a civil marriage.[4] They married through Catholic rites on June 10, 1923.

Author Marisa Rosado describes in her biography an interesting period in the life of the newly married couple. Urged by Don Pedro to continue her studies at Radcliffe College in part due to the financial challenge of maintaining a family home, Doña Laura made her way to New York City and, instead of going directly to Boston, made an unplanned visit to her sister-in-law Filomena. Feeling forced to leave Puerto Rico, Doña Laura questioned Don Pedro's love for her and fell into a depression that affected her health. Following two letters sent by Filomena explaining the situation, Don Pedro wrote a letter to Doña Laura on August 8, 1922 asking her to return to Ponce. By the time it reached its destination, Doña Laura had left to be with her family in Peru.[5]

Continuing to write her husband from Peru, Doña Laura eventually decided to go ahead and continue her studies at Radcliffe College and arrived on campus in October. However, Doña Laura's desire to be with her husband was so great that she immediately wrote to him and explained her desire to discontinue her studies again and wait for him in New York City so they can travel to Puerto Rico together. Don Pedro boarded the SS Ponce on October 25 and arrived in New York City on October 30—when asked for his address in the U.S., he provided 233 West 115th Street.[6] Spending a short time together in New York City, they boarded the SS Porto Rico on November 11 and arrived in San Juan on November 16.[7]

Life As A Family In Puerto Rico

With Don Pedro not earning much in terms of an income, life as a married couple was difficult. In her book *Albizu Campos y la Independencia de Puerto Rico*, Doña Laura reminisced about the community they belonged to sharing the little they had with each other.[8] Don Pedro and Doña Laura went on to have three children together: their son Pedro on March 26, 1924; their daughter Rosa Emilia on August 31, 1925; and their second daughter Laura Esperanza on October 16, 1927. Laura Esperanza was born in Peru after Doña Laura moved there temporarily for about two years.

The family was very much stressed financially, the children even having to share clothing. On several occasions Don Pedro asked friends for money and other items to sustain his family. After one "terrible night with the little girl," he wrote a letter to a friend asking for "a jar of milk of magnesia, a packet of lactose, and five cents of bicarbonate," in addition to "ten dollars, or whatever you can." Other examples of their financial hardship include not being able to host visitors for dinner for lack of food to prepare, and not being able to afford the bus for their son.

On August 30, 1932, the fourth child of Don Pedro—Héctor Manuel—was born of an extra-marital affair with Carmen Aponte Roubert, a woman he had known even before he left Puerto Rico for college. Developing a closer relationship with Carmen after returning to Puerto Rico in 1921, Don Pedro ended their relationship amicably when Laura Meneses arrived in Ponce the following year. Their son Héctor said in an interview that, when he first returned from Harvard, Don Pedro often had lunch at his mother's home. Carmen sometimes left food for him with the secretary at his law office.

Don Pedro and his son Héctor did not really get to know each other until after Don Pedro returned to Puerto Rico in 1947 following a 10-year exile. Many tried to hide Héctor's relationship to Don Pedro due to his prominence as a national figure, but Héctor maintained a positive view of his father even if from a distance. Don Pedro occasionally visited Héctor and even supported him at times. In one instance, following a serious accident and injury playing baseball that doctors initially said would result in the amputation of Héctor's arm, Don Pedro stepped in and was able to arrange a medical operation that saved his arm.

Name	Birthdate	Birthplace	Mother
Pedro Albizu Meneses	March 26, 1924	Puerto Rico	Laura Meneses de Albizu Campos
Rosa Emilia Albizu Meneses	August 31, 1925	Puerto Rico	"
Laura Esperanza Albizu Meneses	October 16, 1927	Peru	"
Héctor Manuel Albizu Aponte	August 30, 1932	Puerto Rico	Carmen 'Lila' Aponte Roubert

Don Pedro's Children

Chapter 10: Choosing A Political Party

Joining The Movement For Independence

Experienced in advocating in support of national liberation struggles, educated in law, trained in military discipline and organization, seasoned in public speaking and debate, and most importantly, deeply committed to serving his country, Don Pedro had significant potential to become a successful political leader. After returning to Puerto Rico in the summer of 1921, he eventually decided to join the *Partido Unión de Puerto Rico*, the only party at the time that had independence as part of its political program. This fact, however, was not the only reason he joined them.

In an interview published in the magazine *Poliedro* on January 8, 1927, Don Pedro explained that upon his return from Harvard there were no political parties that drew his attention.[9] He said that, despite independence being in the Union Party's program, they did not interest him because:

> *"[T]hey cooperated directly with the demolition work directed from Washington instead of sustaining a collective action that would allow us to preserve our wealth as a necessary base to establish our national sovereignty."*

Don Pedro's decision to join the Unionists came as a result of the governorship of Emmet Montgomery Reily, a businessman who held local offices in Texas and Missouri before being appointed governor of Puerto Rico in July 1921.

Nicknamed "Moncho Reyes" by Puerto Ricans, Governor Reily was severely pro-American. He did not allow any flag other than that of the U.S. to be raised in Puerto Rico, stating in his inaugural speech that "while Old Glory floats in the United States, it will continue floating over Puerto Rico." He furthered efforts already underway to have Spanish replaced by English in schools as the language of instruction. He strongly opposed all pro-independence sentiment. Attacking the Union Party in particular, Governor Reily actively worked to remove its members from all governmental positions they held and replace them with pro-American politicians from the U.S. It was in this climate, when the Union Party was under attack and had zero chance of holding positions in the colonial government, that Don Pedro decided to join them.

Don Pedro admitted in his 1927 *Poliedro* interview that:

> *"[I] was seriously mistaken in believing that, out of the pain, a rebel party would be organized. I confused the commotion formed by those who had lost public offices with true rebellion."*

Don Pedro consistently pushed for independence at all Union Party meetings and rallies. In May 1924, after leaders of the Union Party and the pro-statehood *Partido Republicano Puertorriqueño* merged to form the *Alianza Puertorriqueña* in pursuit of "sovereignty inside of the sovereignty of the United States," Don Pedro left the party.

Membership In The Nationalist Party Of Puerto Rico

Just as immediately as he left the Union Party, Don Pedro joined the *Partido Nacionalista de Puerto Rico*. Formed in September 1922 by dissident Union Party members, the Nationalist Party viewed independence as the only option to solve the colonial problem of Puerto Rico. Don Pedro decided not to join the Nationalist Party at first because he perceived it to be divisive, choosing the Union Party instead because of its longer history, much larger and more influential membership, and the fact that it was seemingly in direct conflict with the colonial regime. When Don Pedro joined the Nationalist Party, he quickly began working with his usual intensity.

Ramón Mayoral Barnés, a member of the Nationalist Party's Board of Directors and a resident of Ponce, was surprised to see a young, brilliant lawyer with so much to gain choose to join a party that "cannot offer him anything other than work and sacrifice for the independence of the homeland." Don Pedro attended Nationalist Party meetings, gave lectures, wrote articles, and fully exhibited his leadership potential as a new member of the Party. Perhaps his most important activity was in working with Mayoral Barnés on his newspaper, *El Nacionalista de Ponce*. This newspaper, printed and circulated through the tireless work of Mayoral Barnés, set the Ponce chapter of the Nationalist Party apart from the others.

That same year of 1924, Mayoral Barnés and Don Pedro were both elected by the Party's membership to be their official speakers. Then, for that year's governmental elections, Mayoral Barnés was selected by the Party as their candidate for mayor of Ponce and Don Pedro as their candidate for membership in the House of Representatives. Following their electoral defeat, a Nationalist Party assembly was held on September 6, 1925 and new leadership was elected, with Don Pedro being elected as the Party's vice-president. In this assembly the Party's leadership also approved a resolution to send a representative to countries where they could build solidarity around Puerto Rico's independence movement. After a vote, Don Pedro was elected to be this representative.[10]

In less than a year and a half, owing to his exceptional leadership qualities and sense of duty, Don Pedro joined the Nationalist Party, established his leadership in meetings and conferences, became a key part of their only newspaper, rose to the position of vice-president, and was chosen to represent their cause internationally. What Don Pedro was in the process of introducing to the Party in terms of his approach to developing a bonafide nationalist movement would go on to have a significant impact on Puerto Rico's history. After returning to Puerto Rico from his campaign to build solidarity, which took place from 1927-1930, he was very soon after elected president of the Nationalist Party, beginning his role as the foremost leader of Puerto Rico's independence movement.

Chapter 11: Early Contributions To The Nationalist Party

El Nacionalista De Ponce

El Nacionalista de Ponce, the only publication of the Nationalist Party, served as a significant vehicle for Don Pedro to develop his leadership. When Don Pedro joined the Party in May 1924, Ramón Mayoral Barnés handed over directorship of the newspaper to him. In 1933, during the memorial services for Mayoral Barnés, Don Pedro highlighted the significant amount of work Mayoral Barnés personally put in to print and circulate the newspaper in Puerto Rico and spoke about there being a critical point in 1924 when it seemed the nationalist movement was reduced to three people, including himself and Mayoral Barnés.

As director of the newspaper, Don Pedro used it to directly address and highlight the issues he felt to be of real importance: the colonial condition of Puerto Rico, the global influence of U.S. imperialism, the role of the U.S. military in the domination of Puerto Rico, the activities of the Nationalist Party, and other topics. In the earliest known article written by Don Pedro in the newspaper, published July 13, 1924, he discussed the withdrawal of U.S. troops from Santo Domingo and made a comparison between the imperialist intervention there, in Mexico and Haiti, with the situation in Puerto Rico.

Besides providing a critical analysis of Puerto Rico's colonial situation, a clear focus of the newspaper was also to bring light to the situation in other countries. Connecting the independence struggle in Puerto Rico to the stability and security of Latin America in general was an important part of this for Don Pedro as he saw the two as being intimately connected. The Nationalist Party chapter in Ponce was particularly devoted to this solidarity work, as was clearly shown when, in January 1927, it approved and published a resolution made independent of the larger organization in protest of U.S. military aggressions in Nicaragua. This perspective based on a common struggle among Latin Americans, combined with a desire to act in solidarity, later helped Don Pedro during his political tour of Latin America.

With respect to Don Pedro's political views, *El Nacionalista de Ponce* helped him to contribute and spread the ideals that would define his future leadership within the Party, views in clear distinction to those maintained by the Party's leadership before him. *El Nacionalista de Ponce*, under Don Pedro's directorship, had an important role in publicizing the ideas and attitudes that later influenced the direction of the Nationalist Party. Soon after beginning his tour of Latin America, Don Pedro wrote back to Ponce and expressed his feeling that the newspaper's title no longer fit the vision he had for it. From that point forward the newspaper was titled *El Nacionalista de Puerto Rico*.[11]

Boycotting The Colonial Regime

As a quickly rising leader in the Nationalist Party that also directed a newspaper able to spread his message, Don Pedro wasted no time in elaborating the character and course he felt should define the new nationalist movement. On July 28, 1924, an article was published in *El Nacionalista de Ponce* where he presented his argument that the U.S. government's control over Puerto Rico, as an attack on and denial of its national sovereignty, was illegal.[12] This argument, based on international law, would be a foundational concept Don Pedro repeatedly mentioned.

According to Don Pedro, as published in January 1927 and outlined in notes he made while in Cuba later that year, the Treaty of Paris that ended the Spanish-American War was null and void regarding Puerto Rico. He argued that, because Spain had granted autonomy to Puerto Rico in 1897 and Puerto Rico was not part of the negotiations in Paris:

> *"Spain had no right to cede our country to the United States, and the latter could not demand the handing over of the same for any reason."*[13]

With this understanding that the ruling government in Puerto Rico was illegal, Don Pedro, from the beginning of his membership in the Nationalist Party, called on the Party's members to refrain from holding any kind of public office within the colonial regime. Several nationalists in various towns answered this call.

Honoring The Flag

The most visible aspect of the new kind of leadership Don Pedro represented was based around his insistence that only the Puerto Rican flag, as symbol of the nation, be used at public events of the Nationalist Party. In a Party meeting held in San Juan's Baldorioty Plaza on July 16, 1926, to commemorate the death of José de Diego—attended by some 3,000 people—Don Pedro began his closing speech with a strong denunciation of the presence of the U.S. flag in Puerto Rico.

This moment has been popularly remembered because of Don Pedro's dramatic gesture in response to José Coll y Cuchí[14] who, in his speech, said, "American flag, I salute you because you represent liberty and the first American republic." Don Pedro silently removed each small U.S. flag from the stage, placed them in his jacket pocket, and began to speak, saying:

> *"Flag of the United States, I do not salute you because although it is true that you are the symbol of a free and sovereign nation, in Puerto Rico you represent piracy and pillage."*

As reported on July 24 in *El Nacionalista de Ponce*, Don Pedro continued "by stating that Mr. Coll y Cuchí had been too noble to pay such an eloquent salute to the flag of the United States, when that flag was raised on the backs of black people and continues to be sustained by the slavery of those same unfortunate people and of exploited immigrants from Europe and when it actually is a mourning symbol for all of humanity."

Calling For A Constitutional Convention

In his essay on the 'forging' of Don Pedro's leadership from 1924-1930, historian Amílcar Tirado Avilés highlights the influence of Don Pedro and the "new orientation of nationalism" alluded to by the author of that July article in the following closing statement: "We will attend to every right, that of revolution if necessary, as Albizu Campos rightly said, although for now our Party wants to definitively unmask Yankee imperialism, proposing that the people of Puerto Rico gather immediately to draft the constitution that is to govern the destinies of the Republic of Puerto Rico."[15] What the author's statement reveals is support for Don Pedro's acceptance of revolutionary struggle and the call to hold a constitutional convention to form an independent republic.

This call for political leaders to gather immediately to draft a constitution was another foundational concept[16] that Don Pedro brought to the Nationalist Party. While it was largely ignored at first, it suddenly became a central focus of all the island's main political parties in a rarely discussed period of 1936. Of considerable importance within Don Pedro's views, the call for a constitutional convention can be appreciated as being what Don Pedro believed to be the only diplomatic option to emerge from colonialism as a nation, the convention being an inclusive and democratic national process that could not be controlled by the U.S. government. The non-diplomatic option was revolution.

Don Pedro developed considerable influence in these early years as a member of the Nationalist Party and was beginning to make an impact on the nationalist movement. It was here when he would represent the Party and its cause on a tour of Latin America.

Chapter 12: El Maestro In Latin America

Internationalizing The Nationalist Movement

Don Pedro accepted the mission of representing the Nationalist Party in a tour of Latin America on September 6, 1925, and did not depart from Puerto Rico until June 20, 1927. The significance of the undertaking was not lost on Don Pedro, and he was so committed to making the trip that, due to very little money being raised, he and his wife decided to sell the furniture and other items in their possession to help finance it. He once told her, "If we want our movement to be a liberating movement, we cannot stop ourselves before any obstacle." The personal sacrifice Don Pedro had to make for the trip obviously also included being separated from his family. Doña Laura, who was pregnant, and their two children lived for the duration of his trip with her family in Peru.

In his June 11, 1927 interview in *Los Quijotes*, Don Pedro provided the following analysis of Puerto Rico's colonial situation and the real significance of his upcoming trip:

> *"Our painful situation under the empire of the United States is the situation that North America intends to impose on all our brother peoples of the Continent. Our cause is the Continental cause... If the North American absorption in our land triumphs, the Yankee spirit of conquest will have no restraint."*

Don Pedro also saw his trip as a continuation of the revolutionary work of Puerto Rican patriots like Ramón Emeterio Betances and Eugenio María de Hostos. Such revolutionaries, through their work to free Puerto Rico from imperial control, connected Puerto Rico's struggle with the larger goal of achieving regional unity and security. To achieve this, they sought the formation of a confederation of the various nations of the Antilles. Don

Pedro saw the importance of this Antillean Confederation but also contemplated a larger continental cause. Interestingly, it is precisely in the Antilles—in the Dominican Republic, Haiti, and Cuba—where Don Pedro had the most success during his trip.

Location	*Date(s)*
Departs from Puerto Rico	June 20, 1927
Dominican Republic	June 21 - September 10, 1927
Haiti	September 11-13, 1927
Cuba	September 16 - December 1927
Mexico	December 1927 - February 1928
Cuba (Second time)	February 25 - March 1928
Peru	March 1928 - December 1929
Venezuela	December 1929
Returns to Puerto Rico	January 4, 1930

Don Pedro's Political Tour Of 1927-1930

The Dominican Republic: June 21 - September 10, 1927

When Don Pedro arrived, the Dominican Republic was two years removed from an eight-year military occupation by the United States. As director of a newspaper, Don Pedro had been exchanging correspondence with Dominican patriots on the situation in their respective countries. This relationship made it possible for Don Pedro to be immediately received upon his arrival on June 21 by the Dominican Nationalist Party, the Dominican press, and others. The first action of Don Pedro was to pay a visit to the *Capilla de los Inmortales de la Catedral de Santo Domingo* and pay tribute to the Dominican revolutionaries whose remains were placed there, some of whom had worked with Ramón Emeterio Betances.

In his first interview in the Dominican Republic, Don Pedro stated that his work "must be mostly organizational." He clarified:

> *"It is not my purpose to make beautiful speeches to garner ephemeral applause... I want to leave here, when I go, a living and permanent body that is in charge of reproducing the palpitations of Puerto Rican nationalism outside the homeland."*[17]

During his trip, his work influenced the forming of the *Junta Dominicana Pro-Independencia de Puerto Rico* in Santo Domingo led by Federico Henríquez y Carvajal and Américo Lugo, the *Junta Nacionalista Puertorriqueña* in La Romana organized by Puerto Ricans living in the Dominican Republic, and other organizations in support of Puerto Rico's independence movement in Santiago de los Caballeros and in Puerto Plata.

While in the Dominican Republic, Don Pedro was able to engage directly with the nation's clergy, lawyers, students, journalists, doctors, senators, and other leaders. On one occasion, according to an account by his wife, Don Pedro was received by President Horacio Vásquez. Interestingly, it was also reported in a newspaper article written by Américo Lugo, president of the Dominican Nationalist Party, that "a stenographer sent by the United States Consulate" had been present at meetings with the specific intent of reporting Don Pedro's activities to U.S. intelligence.

Haiti: September 11 - 13, 1927

Departing to Cuba with letters of introduction written by prominent Dominicans to Cuban anti-imperialist activists, Don Pedro made an unscheduled stop in Haiti. The country still under military occupation by the U.S., the captain of his ship begged Don Pedro not to disembark in Puerto Príncipe. Stressing his need to be in solidarity with the Haitian people and defy U.S. authority, Don Pedro was able to get the captain to let him go in the early morning on the condition that he return by 11am.

Don Pedro, who also spoke French, immediately directed a taxi driver to take him to the monument of Jean-Jacques Dessalines, a leader in the Haitian Revolution that became the country's first president in 1804. After paying his respects, Don Pedro asked a cab driver to take him to the home of Pierre Paul, the president of the Haitian Nationalist Party.[18]

Received warmly by Pierre Paul, Don Pedro spoke to him very briefly about the political trip he was on and then returned to his ship. Within the hour, Paul was accompanied by fellow Haitian activist Jolibois Fils to invite Don Pedro to a champagne reception they had hastily organized for him. At this impromptu reception, more than one hundred Haitian nationalists were in attendance, as well as members of the Haitian press, all to give support and attention to the movement for Puerto Rico's independence that Don Pedro represented. Years later, Don Pedro said this was "one of the most emotional moments of my life."

In his brief stop in Haiti, Don Pedro made a memorable impact by defying the U.S. military occupation and setting foot on Haitian soil to engage with the local nationalist movement. Having just come from the Dominican Republic, he not only made a point to speak on the need for Spanish-speaking countries to support Haiti, but he also made a specific call for the patriotic union of Dominicans and Haitians. Of course, long before setting foot in Haiti he had voiced his opposition to the U.S. invasion there. For Don Pedro, Haiti's national independence was an equally important part of the struggle against imperialism in the Caribbean and larger region.

Cuba: September 16 - December 1927

Cuba at this time was under the repressive dictatorship of General Gerardo Machado. Undaunted, Don Pedro arrived and spoke out publicly against the dictatorship. On October 10 he delivered a memorable speech at the statue of Cuban revolutionary José Martí in Havana's *Parque Central*. During his time in Cuba, he developed close ties with Cuban youth and students fighting against the Machado regime. On November 27, the 56th anniversary of the execution by Spanish authorities of eight University of Havana medical students, Don Pedro spoke at the *Mausoleo a los Estudiantes de Medicina* in Havana Cemetery on the significance to Cuba, the Antilles, and the world to have such a university "inspired by the principle of the sacrifice of the innocent."

In the beginning of November, an event was hosted in tribute to Don Pedro by the Athens Club, an Afro-Cuban civic and cultural organization founded in 1917. At the event, Cuban historian Dr. Emilio Roig de Leuchsenring read a declaration drafted in opposition to "the systematic plans employed by the Yankees to destroy the Puerto Rican nationality." This declaration, addressed to the nation of Cuba, was on behalf of the *Junta Nacional Cubana Pro-Independencia de Puerto Rico,* formed following Don Pedro's arrival and presided over by Cuban author Enrique José Varona.

In her biography on Don Pedro, Marisa Rosado uses one story from his trip to Cuba to exemplify his humility and willingness to sacrifice his own comfort in carrying out his patriotic duties. After attending one of his conferences, a group of communist students found it suspicious that Don Pedro did not allow them to accompany him to his hotel. Deciding to follow him and see where he was staying, they found that Don Pedro had been sleeping on a bench in *el Paseo del Prado.* Quickly raising funds, the students were able to pay for a hotel room for part of his stay. Not long after, Don Pedro left Cuba for Mexico due to an increase in repression by the Machado regime ahead of a visit to Cuba by the U.S. President.

Mexico: December 1927 - February 1928

Don Pedro described his time in Mexico as very disappointing. Optimistic and full of hope while he was in Cuba due to leads he had received there, he later wrote to his wife, "it seems that Mexicans abroad did not expect what has happened." Don Pedro's reference was to the violent conflict, known as the Cristeros War, between the Mexican government and the Catholic Church. In response to anti-clerical laws passed by the government that restricted the power of priests, the Cristeros, as they were known, openly opposed the government in violent confrontations. "The atmosphere," Don Pedro said, "is the most hostile found so far."

Despite this atmosphere, Don Pedro was granted an interview with President Plutarco Elías Calles. The interview, however, was postponed twice and, although Don Pedro presented himself for both scheduled meetings, they never happened. According to Don Pedro's wife, he was able to make contact with organizations in Mexico and build a feeling of solidarity between nations, but in general it can be said that his time in Mexico did not achieve the results he hoped for at all.

Cuba: February 25 - March 1928

When Don Pedro was forced to leave Cuba for Mexico due to the repression of the Machado regime, it meant that he was unable to be present for the Sixth Pan-American Conference held in Havana from January 16-20. This conference, at which Puerto Rico was the only Latin American country to not have representation, motivated top Puerto Rican politicians to write President Coolidge, who was in attendance, to express their feeling of humiliation. Now back in Cuba, Don Pedro's sole priority was to take part in another major event being held, the World Congress of the Latin Press.

Attending as a representative of *El Nacionalista de Puerto Rico*, Don Pedro immediately wrote a series of motions, four of which were asking: 1) the Congress issue a statement of protest against U.S. intervention in Latin America; 2) the Congress call on the world press to maintain a campaign against the U.S. military occupations of Haiti and Nicaragua; 3) the Latin press be in solidarity with the struggle to establish the Philippines and Puerto Rico as independent republics; 4) non-Latin newspapers with a presence in Latin America be denied participation in the Congress, as was the case with the United Press International and the Associated Press.

Though receiving support from various delegates—Cubans, South Americans, Belgians, Italians, and others—delegates from France spearheaded an opposition to Don Pedro's motions by arguing that the Congress should be free of politics. The discussion became so intense, with Don Pedro insisting that he be granted the right to have his motions heard, that the president of the Congress adjourned the session and formed smaller committees that met separately in different locations later that day. Despite continued resistance to even reading them, Don Pedro's motions were eventually read and voted on, with none of them passing. Several delegates withdrew their original support at the last moment, later admitting to having been pressured to do so.

Peru: March 1928 - December 1929

Like Mexico, time in Peru did not result in much practical support for Don Pedro and the nationalist movement. The greatest opportunity afforded by his trip to Peru was being able to join his wife and children and meet his daughter Laura Esperanza for the first time. Nevertheless, due to his father-in-law being a Colonel in the Peruvian Army, Don Pedro was at least able to discuss the military situation in Lima at some length. Peru being under the dictatorship of Augusto B. Leguía, Don Pedro is said to have given input into a possible uprising against him.

Taking time to write letters to the nationalist leaders of the Dominican Republic he had connected with, Don Pedro also wrote home to Nationalist Party leadership in Puerto Rico. In these letters he expressed his desire to continue his travels to Argentina and requested the financial assistance to do so. Failing to obtain any additional money or even receive a response, he began preparations for returning to Puerto Rico.

Venezuela: December 1929

On their way to Puerto Rico, Don Pedro and his family stopped in the Venezuelan coastal town of La Guaira for a few weeks. While there, he is said to have visited the capital of Caracas often and to have contacted people working in opposition to the dictatorship of President Juan Vicente Gómez. On one occasion, Don Pedro had the opportunity to deliver a speech against the dictatorial regime in front of the mausoleum of Simón Bolívar. Visiting the birth and resting place of Bolívar was no doubt of great significance to Don Pedro, Bolívar being the initiator of the great historical project of liberating the entirety of Latin America that Don Pedro saw his patriotic work as being a direct continuation of.

Return To Puerto Rico

Don Pedro sacrificed much in order to achieve such considerable success in his solidarity mission to Latin America. Establishing significant contacts in the Dominican Republic, Haiti, and Cuba, he added new life to the historic goal of forming an Antillean Confederation able to block imperialist influence in the region. The organizations in support of Puerto Rico's independence he left in the Dominican Republic and Cuba were a resolute victory. His work in the World Congress of the Latin Press, though neutralized, was important in exposing what were becoming coordinated efforts to prevent any narrative in opposition to U.S. international policies from gaining momentum in the world press. Don Pedro finally made his return to Puerto Rico, with his family, on January 4, 1930, after two and a half years of traveling.[19]

Notes To Chapters 9 - 12

1 Denis, *War Against All Puerto Ricans.*

2 whoisalbizu, *Interview with José Enrique Ayoroa Santaliz.*

3 For more on Doña Laura and her role in Puerto Rico's independence struggle, see Chapter 37.

4 Ancestry.com, *Puerto Rico, Civil Registrations, 1885-2001.*

5 Rosado, *Las Llamas de la Aurora.*

6 Ancestry.com, *New York, U.S., Arriving Passenger and Crew Lists (including Castle Garden and Ellis Island), 1820-1957.*

7 Ancestry.com, *Puerto Rico, U.S, Arriving Passenger and Crew Lists, 1901-1962.*

8 Laura de Albizu Campos, *Albizu Campos y la Independencia de Puerto Rico.*

9 Torres, ed., *Obras Escogidas, Tomo I.*

10 Rosado, *Las Llamas de la Aurora.*

11 Rosado, *Las Llamas de la Aurora.*

12 Torres, ed., *Obras Escogidas, Tomo I.*

13 Albizu-Campos Meneses and Fr. Rodríguez León, eds., *Escritos.*

14 The founder of the Nationalist Party of Puerto Rico.

15 Tirado Avilés, *La Forja de un Líder.*

16 For a more in-depth discussion on the call for a constitutional convention, see Chapter 20.

17 Torres, ed., *Obras Escogidas, Tomo I.*

18 Laura de Albizu Campos, *Albizu Campos y la Independencia de Puerto Rico.*

19 Rosado, *Las Llamas de la Aurora.*

Fourth Period — First Nationalist Party Era

Chapter 13: The Start Of A New Era

Marking A New Era Of Struggle

Returning to Puerto Rico on January 4, 1930, without fanfare, Don Pedro set to work reestablishing his law practice and reorganizing *El Nacionalista de Puerto Rico*, which had stopped being published in his absence. He also resumed his political work, attending meetings and conferences, conducting interviews, and writing articles for newspapers. Without a doubt, Don Pedro's return became a turning point in Puerto Rico's history. Juan Antonio Corretjer once wrote, it is here that "The most legendary career of any public man Puerto Rico has known begins to form."[1]

At the Nationalist Party assembly held May 11, 1930, in the *Ateneo Puertorriqueño* of San Juan, Don Pedro was confirmed as their new president. At the assembly he had the opportunity to address the representatives of other political parties in attendance. Following remarks made by representatives of the *Partido Liberal de Puerto Rico*, formerly the Union Party, the *Partido Socialista Constitucional*, and the *Alianza Puertorriqueño*, Don Pedro said:

> "We are united on fundamental questions and divided by tactical questions of a transitory nature. Therefore I would like to see realized the unity of all the parties for the immediate recognition of the independence of Puerto Rico."

Don Pedro spoke extensively on his travels in Latin America, issuing a severe critique of the behavior of Nationalist Party leadership during his absence. Besides failing to provide him financial assistance to travel more, leadership had allowed the Party to become disorganized. Even worse in his view, on one occasion leadership accepted an invitation to *La Fortaleza* by the appointed governor at the time, Theodore Roosevelt, where they shared space and niceties with various colonial authorities and leadership from other political parties. To this Don Pedro said:

> *"A frank and definitive nationalist ideology must be postulated against the invaders. There is no margin for a fraternal and solidary attitude towards the enemies of the homeland."*

Though receiving cheers, Don Pedro's bold statements caused the founder of the Nationalist Party, José Coll y Cuchí, and others, to walk out of the assembly—they eventually also left the Party. Finally confirmed as the Party's new president in the early morning hours, Don Pedro made his inaugural statement, saying:

> *"Let us carry out an intense work of refined nationalism with a defined orientation and program of action... An optimistic philosophy must inform all our actions. Raining on our people is a pessimistic doctrine that demoralizes and cowards them and that we must tackle at all times. It is necessary to raise the public spirit of Puerto Rico and tell it that it can become what it wants and conquer its independence if its will so desires."*

The audience standing on their feet, Don Pedro asked them to raise one hand in the air and then said:

> *"Let us solemnly swear here that we will defend the nationalist ideal and that we will sacrifice our property and our life if necessary for the independence of our homeland."*

The 1932 Election Campaign

At the assembly in which Don Pedro was confirmed as president, the Nationalist Party also agreed on the immediate focus of their work. Their program stated: "The immediate suppression of North American colonialism cannot be postponed, and the Party commits to celebrate the

Constitutional Convention that establishes in Puerto Rico the government of a free, sovereign and independent republic, as soon as it receives the vote of the majority."[2]

With this program, the Party began an energetic campaign focused on securing the 'vote of the majority' in the elections.[3] Their campaign motto was "*¡Valor y Sacrificio!*" Under Don Pedro's leadership, however, Party members only ran for positions dependent on public votes and did not consider positions appointed by the U.S. president or other colonial officials. Neither did they enter into agreements with other parties.[4]

Besides public meetings, rallies, and their own or other newspapers publishing their articles, the Party found an extremely effective tool for campaigning in the radio. Almost every Sunday night Don Pedro utilized the radio to broadcast speeches widely listened to in homes, shops, and clubs all over Puerto Rico. In the main plaza of San Juan an amplifier was used that attracted a huge crowd of listeners. At the end of 1931, several months before the election, individuals aligned with American interests succeeded in getting the radio corporation to cease transmissions of Don Pedro. Around this same time, the newspaper *El Mundo*, which had the largest circulation among newspapers in Puerto Rico, also began to limit the publication of articles written by Nationalist Party members.

With the Nationalist Party effectively censored in the media, the campaign of every other party, all allied with U.S. interests in some way, was now all the public were exposed to. After the elections were held in November 1932, Don Pedro said the following:

> "*In these elections that we have just witnessed, the factions of the government have resorted to all methods to raise the lowest passions in the masses, resorting to all forms of bribery. Something unheard of has been used: the kidnapping of voters.*"

Indeed, in addition to the buying and selling of votes, people in the countryside were offered transportation to voting locations but then brought to warehouses, corrals, slaughterhouses, and other places and prevented from leaving until all the voting was over.

The Nationalist Party was defeated in the elections and Don Pedro received a total of about five thousand votes. He reacted by saying:

> *"Five thousand nationalists have responded to the proclamation to immediately establish the republic! If the majority had responded to this patriotic clarion call, the Constitutional Convention of the Republic would be gathered at this time... The Liberation Army, which has 5,000 places, is constituted under the motto: ¡Valor y Sacrificio!"*

The experience, Don Pedro argued, made it very clear that the electoral arena was not the proper venue for the independence movement. He did not want to take part in the elections in the first place but respected the decision of the majority in the Party that did and went along with it after voicing his opposition. The election results allowed Don Pedro to now argue for a different approach. In his view, "The victory of Puerto Ricans over Puerto Ricans is the defeat of the homeland," and so never again would the Party take part in an election in Puerto Rico. The electoral boycott[5] now became a principle of the struggle.

Chapter 14: Two Notable Events Of 1932

The Nefarious Dr. Rhoads

In the middle of the electoral campaign, Puerto Rico became the site of a medical scandal brought to public attention by Don Pedro. On November 12, 1931, young nationalist Luis Baldoni Martínez reported early to his job as a laboratory assistant in San Juan's Presbyterian Hospital and noticed an envelope placed next to a microscope. Deciding to open it, he found a letter written and signed by Dr. Cornelius Rhoads, a physician working at the hospital through a research project funded by the Rockefeller Foundation to investigate anemia and sprue in Puerto Rico.

In the letter, Dr. Rhoads said the following on Puerto Ricans: "They are beyond doubt the dirtiest, laziest, most degenerate and thievish race of men ever inhabiting this sphere. It makes you sick to inhabit the same island with them. They are even lower than Italians. What the island needs is not public health work but a tidal wave or something to totally exterminate the population. It might then be livable."

He went further and admitted: "I have done my best to further the process of extermination by killing off 8 and transplanting cancer into several more. The latter has not resulted in any fatalities so far... The matter of consideration for the patients' welfare plays no role here—in fact all physicians take delight in the abuse and torture of the unfortunate subjects."

After one month passed, Baldoni Martínez decided to make its contents known. On January 2, 1932, he went before a notary public, signed an affidavit in connection with his discovery of the letter, and provided both to the Nationalist Party. Immediately recognizing its significance, Don

Pedro quickly went about publicizing the letter. He sent copies of it, along with the affidavit, to newspapers in Puerto Rico, foreign governments, and the Vatican. The newspaper *El Día* even submitted the documents to the attorney general. When news became known through the New York Times that an investigation had been ordered by then-Governor of Puerto Rico James Beverley, Dr. Rhoads wrote to him expressing that the letter was "a fantastic and playful composition written entirely for my own diversion and intended as a parody."[6]

The prosecutor assigned to the case, José Ramón Quiñones, commented that Dr. Rhoads is either "mentally ill or unscrupulous." His official report to the governor confirmed that, in experiments performed as part of the Rockefeller Foundation-funded project, thirteen people had died, eight of them having been treated by Dr. Rhoads. Nevertheless, by February 14 Dr. Rhoads was cleared of all charges, bringing many to question the loyalties and legitimacy of the justice system in Puerto Rico.[7] Dr. Rhoads later received awards and acclaim for establishing chemical weapons labs for the U.S. Army during World War 2, and for serving as the first director of the Sloan-Memorial Kettering Institute for Cancer Research. He also appeared on the cover of Time Magazine.[8]

Manuel Rafael Suárez Díaz

A few months after the scandal with Dr. Rhoads, the Nationalist Party held an event to honor the birthday of Puerto Rican patriot José de Diego on April 16 in San Juan's *Plaza de Armas*. At the same time, the Senate was discussing a bill that proposed to convert the single-starred flag of Puerto Rico, which at the time was only used by nationalists and independence supporters, into the official flag of the colony. In the middle of his speech, Don Pedro was approached by a nationalist who had just arrived from the capitol building to tell him of the news.

When Don Pedro brought the news to his audience, he asked, "What are we going to do now?" The crowd replied, "Let's stop it!" According to a police estimate cited by the New York Times, Don Pedro led a crowd of about 1,500 people to the capitol building just one half-mile away. Arming themselves with sticks and rocks, the crowd chanted "*¡Viva la República! ¡Abajo los bandoleros!*" Notified of the coming protestors, the police lined up in front of the capitol building and tried in vain to deny their entry as the protestors pushed through and made their way to the stairs leading to the legislative floor. The entire time police and protestors were fighting outside, police with their clubs and protestors with whatever they had picked up on the way.

Inside of the building the weight of the protestors being pushed and wrestled by police caused part of the balcony to collapse, dropping the people some 25 feet to the floor below. Eleven people were taken to the hospital, Don Pedro was immediately arrested on charges of inciting a riot, and the bill to adopt the flag was never approved. A high school student, Manuel Rafael Suárez Díaz, died in the fall.[9]

At his trial, Don Pedro tried to get the case dismissed by arguing against the authority of U.S. courts in Puerto Rico. When this was overruled, he presented a defense and succeeded. His case was dismissed on June 23.[10]

The death of Suárez Díaz was held in great significance by Don Pedro and the Nationalist Party. In a speech years later, on April 16, 1950, Don Pedro reflected on the impact it had on him personally, saying, "There I found myself in the most bitter sadness of my life, a mother had lost her only son... a hero." Historian Marisa Rosado summed up the impact his death had on the Party, writing, "The nationalists since then claim Suárez Díaz as their first martyr and conceive the flag as consecrated with his blood."

The following year after the event at the capitol, Don Pedro delivered a speech in the presence of Suárez Díaz' mother and took a moment to acknowledge her as "the first martyr mother of the homeland of this generation." The speech, publicized in *El Mundo* on May 12, 1933, was given on what Don Pedro declared to be "the Day of the Consecration of the Flag of Puerto Rico."[11]

Chapter 15: Leading A Principled Movement

Complete Non-Collaboration With The Empire

The principle of non-collaboration with the colonial regime was promoted by Don Pedro as soon as he returned to Puerto Rico from his university studies ten years earlier. It was his belief in it that brought him to join the Union Party when its members were being removed from and actively prevented from taking positions in government. As already mentioned, when a majority of the Party expressed their desire to enter the 1932 elections, Don Pedro only ran after first voicing his opposition.

Following the elections, Don Pedro led the Nationalist Party using the principle of complete non-collaboration with the colonial regime. Instead of the Party just refusing to accept governmental positions dependent on direct appointment, the Party would now refuse to serve in any position within the colonial government, appointed or not. The Party began attracting even more militant supporters of Puerto Rican nationalism.

A few months after the election Don Pedro said the following:

> *"We do not want cowards in our ranks, not a single one. We do not want the undisciplined in our ranks, because indiscipline is a cancer worse than treason. Men and women who do not know how to obey do not know how to command either. The work of a people is forged with labor, with virtue, and with courage, and that is the message that the names of De Diego and Suárez Díaz leave us."*

Supporting Workers' Struggles

In a February 1930 interview, Don Pedro made a statement about the ownership of wealth that he maintained throughout his leadership:

"It is necessary to repeat always and at all times: that the land, the communication routes, the maritime fronts and everything that represents real wealth in Puerto Rico must belong to Puerto Ricans."

After the first year of his presidency, Don Pedro showed his interest in directly supporting the struggles of workers and began to be more proactive in using his position as a political leader to do so.

In January 1931, Don Pedro made his first call for workers, in this case farmers, to conduct a strike. With small- and medium-sized farmers facing foreclosure by the Federal Land Bank of Baltimore for not being able to pay their mortgage loans, he urged them to hold onto their lands at all costs and conduct a tax strike. Taking his advice, when Internal Revenue agents came to collect, the farmers refused to give any money.

In 1933, Don Pedro led an even more successful strike that put Puerto Rico in a virtual standstill. Protesting the high prices of gasoline, public transportation workers, again through the influence of Don Pedro, refused to work and achieved a significant victory against U.S.-owned gas companies. It was also the first time that troops were deployed for 'riot prevention' by the government in response to Don Pedro's activities.[12]

Also leading a successful protest against low-quality, high-priced bread, which he attributed to the low quality of flour being imported, the most significant involvement Don Pedro would have in a labor struggle came in January 1934. Within the extremely lucrative, U.S. dominated sugar production industry, the *Federación Libre de Trabajadores*—the economic component of the *Partido Socialista de Puerto Rico* and affiliate of the American Federation of Labor—signed an agreement with industry leadership that was not in the interest of the actual workers of the industry. In response, the workers of the *Central Fajardo* sugar company declared a strike to demand, among other things, a higher salary.

The strikers visited Don Pedro's humble home made of wood in Río Piedras to ask that he lead their strike. On January 15, newspapers announced that Don Pedro accepted the request of the strikers to head their efforts. They were equally in protest of their union leaders as the contract they signed. With the strike taking place across the South and Northeast of Puerto Rico, paralyzing the industry's largest sugar producers, Don Pedro's leadership caused a panic within the colonial regime. The police were increased in size, armed with machine guns and automatic weapons, and sent to the factories on strike to intimidate workers. Despite this, over the next three weeks, Don Pedro visited and spoke in almost all parts of Puerto Rico. Eventually, the workers secured a historic victory that included the sought-after wage increase.[13]

The Nullity Of The Treaty Of Paris

Possibly the most important principle held by Don Pedro, on which it can be argued all the characteristics of his leadership were grounded, is 'the nullity of the Treaty of Paris.' Having first published the concept in *El Nacionalista de Ponce* in January 1927, Don Pedro repeated it during his travels in Latin America and then expanded it as president of the Nationalist Party. Its most detailed explanation was given in October 1935 as part of a legal case[14] Don Pedro brought to the U.S. Court of Appeals in Boston as defense attorney for Luis F. Velázquez, a member of the Nationalist Party.[15]

Don Pedro's argument starts with the Charter of Autonomy granted to Puerto Rico by Spain in 1897. This charter, in addition to establishing an insular government in Puerto Rico, contained an article stating, "Once the present Constitution for the islands of Cuba and Puerto Rico has been approved by the Courts of the Kingdom, it may not be modified except by virtue of a law and at the request of the Insular Parliament."

Don Pedro then points out the fact that the Treaty of Paris signed in 1898, which resulted in Spain ceding Puerto Rico to the United States, "was not negotiated by Puerto Rican plenipotentiaries, nor was it ratified by the Parliament of Puerto Rico in accordance with the Autonomous Charter." The conclusion to be made, he argued, was that "Said Treaty is null and void as far as Puerto Rico is concerned."

This clear, well-articulated understanding of Puerto Rico's situation was formulated with the help of his training as a lawyer and exposure to international law during his time at Harvard. For Don Pedro, because the negotiations of the Treaty of Paris violated the rights of Puerto Rico under the Charter of Autonomy, the U.S. colonial structure in Puerto Rico was illegitimate and all opposition to it was justified.

In his view, Puerto Rico was a legally constituted nation that was militarily intervened by the United States. What he sought was to reclaim and restore Puerto Rico's sovereignty and allow its national development to continue with the recognition and support of the rest of Latin America and the larger international community.

Chapter 16: Developing A People's Conscience

Breaking With The Colonial Mindset

In his May 11, 1930 inaugural speech as president of the Nationalist Party, Don Pedro spoke on the need to adopt an optimistic philosophy and to actively resist the pessimism prevalent among the people. He said:

> *"[I]t is necessary that we bring a moral infusion to our people so that they may believe again in their destiny and in their possibilities."*

Essentially, he was talking about a psychological transformation undoing the colonial mindset that feeds the belief that the people are incapable of gaining, much less maintaining, independence. Don Pedro was very aware that, as he said on September 23, 1930, "All empires hold propaganda in their colonies to maintain the myth of their superiority."

Within the context of Puerto Rico's colonial situation, Don Pedro viewed nationalism as a force that developed a people's conscience in connection to values based on the exercise of freedom. In a 1930 speech in Ponce, he said:

> *"Nationalism is the force that stands against any power that denies us personality. It is a movement that aspires to awaken the forces of wisdom in the people... it is the nationality on a footing to rescue their sovereignty and save this people for the higher values of life."*

For Don Pedro, the purpose of the nationalist movement was more than achieving material progress, it was about an elevation of spirit. Material progress would serve to support the development of the national personality. This development of Puerto Rico's national personality—of its nationhood—was being denied by colonialism and was the people's right.

Honoring The Spirit Of Lares

This development of the people's conscience was of primary importance to Don Pedro. Many of the nationalist traditions he introduced had a profound effect in supporting this process, and some of these traditions are intact today. As soon as he became president of the Nationalist Party, he started the tradition of celebrating the birthday of important Puerto Rican historical figures—José de Diego, Ramón Emeterio Betances, Eugenio María de Hostos, and others. He also increased the level of respect given the Puerto Rican flag, insisting that the U.S. flag not be displayed alongside it and recognizing Manuel Rafael Suárez Díaz as a martyr who died defending its honor. Probably the most significant nationalist tradition he started centered around *El Grito de Lares*.

Though militarily defeated, the revolutionary uprising against Spain on September 23, 1868 that saw the first declaration of Puerto Rico as an independent republic held great symbolic importance for nationalists. To Don Pedro, it was "the Day of the Heroes and Martyrs of Independence."

In 1930, Don Pedro started a tradition that continues today where, every September 23rd, people make a "pilgrimage" to the "Holy Land" and "Altar of the Homeland" that is the town of Lares. The purpose of this pilgrimage was, and is, to pay homage to "the heroes of our liberty." Don Pedro saw the pilgrimage as more than just an opportunity to pay homage. He saw it as an opportunity to receive the inspiration of courage and sacrifice that the revolutionary heroes of Lares embodied.[16]

Don Pedro gave emphasis to the historical importance of the participants of *El Grito de Lares* and the symbols associated with the event. These symbols included the first flag of Puerto Rico sewn by Mariana Bracetti used that day and which is the current flag of Lares, and the national

78

anthem *La Borinqueña* written by Lola Rodríguez de Tió for the revolution and which is still sung by independence supporters. These figures and symbols were employed as a powerful connection to the spirit of revolution represented by *El Grito de Lares*. When the last living survivor of *El Grito*—110-year-old Don Pedro Angleró—passed away[17] on October 16, 1931, the Nationalist Party issued a statement calling for nine days of mourning, asking all chapters of the Party to pay religious tribute and fly the Puerto Rican flag at half-mast.[18]

Controlling Public Education

The speeches and articles of Don Pedro, as well as the traditions he started around Puerto Rican figures and historical events, especially related to *El Grito de Lares*, were rich with educational content. They allowed for the general public to gain exposure to a repressed history and narrative that made possible the development of a sense of self-awareness and dignity at the core of the nationalist movement. To combat the propaganda put forth by U.S. and colonial officials, Don Pedro's very words and leadership became a kind of public education that taught the values of courage, sacrifice, and revolution.

While such is true, there was still an education system under U.S. control that would not dare teach the people their own history. On October 18, 1930, during a tribute paid to him by the Cultural Society of the College of Laws, Don Pedro took the opportunity to criticize the system of education and said:

> "The school can serve to build as well as destroy. We must seek the purpose that is pursued through teaching. Education cannot be an instrument of domination; education should develop informed men that are of a patriotic approach and not servants of the prevailing regime."

Don Pedro proved to have a considerable influence on young people and students. Many of them became members of the Nationalist Party, and others even established student organizations that both supported Don Pedro and became independently active around issues such as university reform and the use of Spanish as the language of instruction in schools instead of the imposed English. Don Pedro even played a significant role in 1933 during a strike at the University of Mayagüez where students had a confrontation with police.

Chapter 17: Organizing A Nation

Building A National Movement

The Nationalist Party under the leadership of Don Pedro became a bona fide national movement. As he traveled across the territory of Puerto Rico educating the masses about their colonial situation, the heroes and symbols that define their history, and the actions they could take to secure their freedom, he led the organization of a movement.

The level of organization achieved, unparalleled in the history of the Nationalist Party or any movement for independence in Puerto Rico, would become a serious threat to the colonial regime. It was quickly a real national movement with representation throughout Puerto Rico.

The Party was organized with a governing body at its head known as the *Junta Nacional*, presided over by Don Pedro and the top leadership of the Party. Under this body, the Party was organized into *Juntas Municipales* based in the various municipalities, each junta having its own board of directors in charge of membership, activities, and other matters. A declassified document shows how well-organized the Party was in 1936.[19]

Based on an investigation made from February 10-20, 1936, FBI agents concluded, "the Nationalist Party Movement is well spread throughout the Island of Puerto Rico. In each locality there exist a Junta locals (local council) with the respective officers." The document goes on to provide the names for the president, vice-president, treasurer, secretary, and other positions in 33[20] municipalities. The list, for some reason, does not include other municipalities that were also known to have an organized Nationalist Party presence, such as Ponce, Jayuya, and Caguas.

The Liberation Army Of Puerto Rico

In an interview conducted while in the Dominican Republic published in *El Mundo* on July 16, 1927, Don Pedro said the following:

> *"Puerto Rico has to pose a serious crisis to the colonial administration in order to be attended to in its demand... A nation like the United States, with enormous national and international problems, does not have time to attend to submissive and servile men. Required is the formation of an organization that encompasses the entire people of Puerto Rico and that definitively breaks with the colonial regime, and asks of the free nations the recognition of our independence in order to achieve the concentration of the American mind on our situation."*

This was Don Pedro's mindset as the new president of the Nationalist Party. It remained so for as long as he held the position.

The possibility of needing to commit to an armed revolution was another aspect of Don Pedro's views that he felt the people, in support of their liberation, must also be open to. He spoke more openly about this following the 1932 elections. Not only was he inspired by the 1916 Easter Uprising in Ireland, but he was committed to upholding the example set forth by the revolutionary heroes of *El Grito de Lares*.

On March 23, 1931, the *Asociación Patriótica de Jóvenes Puertorriqueños* was formed, the precursor to the *Cuerpo de Cadetes de la República* formed the following year. The purpose of this organization, he explained in 1936, was "to increase discipline, improve the physical condition of all Party members and increase their devotion to the homeland."

As outlined in Nelson Denis' book centered around the Nationalist Insurrection of 1950, the Corps of Cadets "underwent a full training program that included marching, field tactics, self-defense, and survival.

Since they had no firearms, they trained and marched with wooden rifles." The Cadets had over a dozen recruiting stations throughout Puerto Rico, were active in twenty-one towns, had a membership of over 10,000 by 1936, and were divided into fifty companies of two hundred cadets, "each with a command structure of sergeants, captains, colonels, and one commander in chief, Raimundo Díaz Pacheco."[21] They conducted weekly military drills and their military formations were a regular presence at Nationalist Party parades and events.

Known for marching with the flags of Puerto Rico[22] and the Nationalist Party, and dressing in their uniform of white pants and black shirts, the Corps of Cadets had their name changed to the *Ejército Libertador de Puerto Rico* on December 8, 1935. The Liberation Army also had a female component that began as the *Hijas de la Libertad* in 1932 and was renamed the *Cuerpo de Enfermeras* in 1935. They developed out of the desire women had to become active participants in the struggle, and the desire of leaders to provide women with free medical training as nurses. The Daughters of Liberty received training from actual registered nurses, some of which were also members, and marched in public events in military formation alongside the Corps of Cadets.[23]

Student And Worker Organizations

The Liberation Army, though committed to the militant nationalist struggle that Don Pedro led under the motto "Valor y Sacrificio," was not meant to pose a definitive military threat to the U.S. government. Despite this, the Liberation Army was the target of investigations and infiltration by U.S. agents from its inception. What would really threaten and strike fear into the U.S. government, however, were the organizations outside of the Party that developed as a result of Don Pedro's example and leadership. Many of these organizations adopted his moral leadership and connected their struggles to the political situation existing in Puerto Rico, adopting the call for sovereignty and independence as the purpose behind their efforts.

In December 1932 the *Federación Nacional de Estudiantes Puertorriqueños* was organized, going on to play a key role in a 1933 university strike that saw incidents of direct confrontation between students and police. They also formed the first student congresses to take place on a national level in Puerto Rico. The Federation, which was made up of high school and university students, maintained support for Don Pedro and the goal of independence for Puerto Rico while fighting for university reform, university autonomy, the use of Spanish in schools, and cultural exchange with other Latin American countries.[24]

What had the most intimidating effect on the United States was Don Pedro's leadership role during the strike of sugar cane workers in January 1934, discussed briefly in a previous chapter. Important to note is that, after accepting their request to lead their strike, Don Pedro motivated the workers to eventually create the *Asociación de Trabajadores Puertorriqueños*. The set of demands won under Don Pedro's leadership, which included the doubling of worker salaries, came despite the presence of a newly militarized police at demonstrations.

With U.S. officials becoming greatly alarmed by this disturbance in one of their major sources of profit, and Puerto Rican police supplied with personnel and equipment for use in what had become a genuine conflict between the empire and the Nationalist Party, it was here that an environment of terror, and patriotic resistance to that terror, fully emerged.

Chapter 18: The War Against Nationalists

Developing A Military Regime

When strikes across several industries in Puerto Rico broke out in 1933 and the U.S. government was put on high alert, the U.S. administration, headed by President Roosevelt, made several appointments intended to take control of the situation and enforce order. The first appointment, on October 1, 1933, was former U.S. Army Colonel Francis E. Riggs as chief of police in Puerto Rico. Prior to this, Colonel Riggs worked in Nicaragua advising that country's future dictator Anastasio Somoza. Just a few months later, Somoza ordered the assassination of Augusto Sandino, the nationalist leader of the opposition to him.[25]

The next appointment, on January 12, 1934, saw former U.S. Army General Blanton Winship become governor of Puerto Rico. Former Governor of Puerto Rico James Beverly wrote a letter of recommendation for Winship to the Bureau of Insular Affairs on January 1st, saying, "I strongly encourage the next governor to be an Army officer... He must be someone with a lot of experience who knows how to gauge and handle delicate situations and who has the necessary toughness to fulfill his duty, the same if it is favored by public opinion or not."

In addition to these appointments of two former Army officers, a new U.S. attorney for the District of Puerto Rico was appointed, Aaron Cecil Snyder, as well as a new judge for the District Court of Puerto Rico, Robert A. Cooper.[26]

Now under the leadership of Riggs, the police of Puerto Rico were armed with military-grade weapons.[27] Adding to this tense climate, Riggs was quoted in *El Mundo* on February 5, 1934 as saying, "If the Police have to use their weapons and shoot in self defense or to maintain order, they will do so with effective results." The order he received from Governor Winship was even more explicit: "In front of the nationalists, always shoot to kill." A militarized regime had been created, with new appointees in the legal structure able to control the exercise of law at the highest insular levels. The FBI also sent more agents with specific orders to infiltrate and conduct non-stop surveillance on all nationalists.

Bribery, Internal Opposition, And Violent Confrontation

In the middle of the strike, on January 18, 1934, Don Pedro accepted a lunch invitation from Riggs. Don Pedro's wife claimed Riggs stated, "that due to his position he could not act publicly, but that he could help financially, for example, contributing with one hundred and fifty thousand dollars for Nationalism." Juan Antonio Corretjer, however, denied that this offer was given, saying such a bribe "presupposes weakness in the one to whom the offer is made," and that Riggs knew Don Pedro was not someone who could be bribed. As for what Don Pedro himself said about the two-hour meeting, he told the press very simply that it was of a personal nature.

Due to the increasing militancy of Don Pedro's leadership, this period is when those in disagreement with the direction he was leading the Party began to leave or, worse, conspire against Don Pedro. The first significant case was tied to the July 1934 visit of U.S. President Roosevelt to Mayagüez. Declaring him "persona non grata," Party leadership tried to organize a protest opposing his arrival with the local Mayagüez chapter. The leadership in Mayagüez, however, did not support the initiative and ended up leaving the Party to form their own separate organization.

The summer of 1935 saw the exposure of an even more serious kind of internal opposition, this time from the Party's Santurce chapter. Invited to a private meeting organized by members of the Party, Ramón S. Pagán, then the treasurer of the Nationalist Party, was surprised to find the agenda of the meeting was the continuation of discussions already begun on how to assassinate Don Pedro. These members, beyond being opponents of the path the Party was on, also appeared to have been encouraged by elements of the colonial government.[28]

Juan Antonio Corretjer was later quoted in *El Imparcial* saying plots against Don Pedro had begun to be uncovered in June 1935. Don Pedro spoke of an effort to plant explosives in Party offices during a meeting in August with the *Junta Nacional* and *Juntas Municipales*. The purpose of this effort, he said, was to create a reason to conduct raids on the homes and arrests of Party members. With the Santurce chapter being the focus of this conspiracy, much of their leadership was expelled from the Party.

Because of the death threats he faced, Don Pedro moved his family to Aguas Buenas in 1935. In her book *Albizu Campos y la Independencia de Puerto Rico*, Doña Laura wrote about agents of the U.S. military conducting information-gathering operations around their residence there. She also wrote about the attempted assaults on their home. With armed guards from the Nationalist Party posted 24-hours a day, on at least four occasions they opened fire on approaching vehicles and repelled attempts to firebomb Don Pedro's home. In one of these night attempts, Don Pedro, armed with a revolver, led his family across the farmland they lived on to the more populated part of town for safety.

The Massacre At Río Piedras

Despite the bribery, internal opposition, and violent confrontation that existed and led a number of members to leave or be expelled from the Party, the activities commemorating *El Grito de Lares* on September 23,

1935 made very clear that the Nationalist Party was still strong, organized, and committed. The very next month, on October 24, 1935, the Nationalist Party was targeted by the colonial regime. A police shooting resulted in the death of four nationalists, including Ramón S. Pagán, and one innocent bystander, with a fifth nationalist being wounded.[29]

A few days before, on October 20, Don Pedro delivered a speech over the radio in which he severely denounced what he found to be a wave of assimilation in the University of Puerto Rico. He felt that the influence of U.S. imperialism was creating cowards and traitors among the student body, and that students ought to be courageous and patriotic in the face of imperialism. Following his speech, and despite applause from political leaders and others who heard his speech, a campaign started by a group of students collected signatures in support of a protest at the university where Don Pedro would be declared "Student Enemy Number One." The effort was denounced by the National Federation of Puerto Rican Students as an effort supported by colonial elements to create a conflict where Nationalist Party members could be arrested.

The students in opposition to Don Pedro notified police of their intention to hold the assembly and requested their security outside the campus. When nationalists arrived at the campus the morning of the assembly, their car was intercepted by police. After a brief confrontation, several policemen opened fire on the vehicle killing three of the four occupants. Witnesses claimed police were screaming, "Don't let them leave alive!" Immediately after, as police were transporting a wounded policeman, a bomb struck their car. Giving chase to a suspect, the police engaged him in a shootout. When the suspect, another nationalist, ran out of bullets and began to surrender, the police shot and killed him. The event, since it took place at the Río Piedras campus of the University of Puerto Rico, became known as the Río Piedras Massacre.

The massacre was widely denounced. Pro-statehood political leader Rafael Martínez Nadal placed blame on the University of Puerto Rico administration. He criticized their decision to allow for a political meeting to declare Don Pedro "Student Enemy Number One" to be held on an educational campus when the dissatisfaction of the students could have been expressed in so many other ways. Chief of Police Riggs, on the other hand, declared in a press conference "war, war without end" against the Nationalist Party.

Chapter 19: Responding To Colonial Violence

Reactions To The Río Piedras Massacre

The reactions to the Río Piedras Massacre were significant. The wake for the fallen nationalists was attended by as many as 8,000 people. At the wake, Don Pedro delivered a passionate speech denouncing the massacre and held Chief of Police Riggs responsible for ordering policemen to the Río Piedras campus with specific orders to kill. To end his speech, Don Pedro made a gesture that, as author Marisa Rosado puts it, "divided the history of Puerto Rico in two: before Albizu Campos and after Albizu Campos."[30] With the participation of those present, Don Pedro proclaimed:

> *"Here the history of all times is repeated: the freedom of the Homeland is acquired with our blood and also with the blood of the Yankees. We come here to take an oath so that this murder does not go unpunished. The Homeland's history does not know of such a serious act of murder, of such supreme cowardice. Raise your hand up, all you who believe to be free. We all swear that murder will not live on in Puerto Rico."*

At the next Nationalist Party general meeting, on October 30, 1935, the Party re-elected Don Pedro as president and responded in kind to the declaration of war made by Riggs to the press: "War, war, war against the Yankees."[31] At this meeting the Party approved a resolution calling for "defensive confrontation." Speaking to this, Don Pedro proclaimed to everyone present:

> *"You have to discipline yourself, you have to be aware of what defense is. The duty of every nationalist is to arm himself well, not with weapons that serve to scratch teeth, but with firearms that shoot well. No nationalist should be allowed to be searched on the street. An improper search is an attack on personal dignity and can be repelled by killing. No nationalist will be unarmed!"*

With this, the Nationalist Party defiantly and definitively adopted armed struggle, beginning a new period in its history. The Party went further and declared military service in the Liberation Army mandatory for all Party members.

Hiram Rosado And Elías Beauchamp

On February 23, 1936, the pledge made to not allow the murder at Río Piedras go unpunished was fulfilled. Following his normal attendance at Sunday mass in San Juan's Cathedral, Chief of Police Riggs got into his car to return home and was fired upon twice by 24-year-old nationalist Hiram Rosado. As his gun jammed, Rosado was prevented from escaping and arrested. At that point another nationalist, 27-year-old Elías Beauchamp, dressed impeccably in all white, approached Riggs without raising any suspicion and said that he witnessed everything. As police arrived and began to take Hiram Rosado to the police station, Riggs invited Beauchamp to ride in his car with him to provide testimony.

Once in the car, Beauchamp produced a pistol and fired twice on Riggs, killing him with a shot to the head and then fleeing the scene. Beauchamp was soon captured in a nearby warehouse. Violently arrested, he told the police he would not shoot on his fellow Puerto Ricans and confessed that he had killed Riggs in retaliation for the Río Piedras massacre. Both Rosado and Beauchamp were taken to the nearby police station.[32]

After failing to reach the governor by phone, one of the policemen got hold of Colonel Cole, commander of the 65th Infantry Regiment. Informed of Riggs' killing, Col. Cole asked if Rosado and Beauchamp were still alive. The policeman hung up and took the question as an order to kill the prisoners. Thus, not long after arriving at the police station, both Rosado and Beauchamp were shot and killed in one of the rooms.

Police tried to justify their actions by claiming the two nationalists tried to seize weapons stored in the room. Questioned by reporters, this justification was proved to be without merit. With news of the event spreading fast, the tense situation resulted in another nationalist, Ángel Mario Martínez, being shot and killed by police later that day in Utuado during a search of his car.

The killing of Rosado and Beauchamp in police custody was widely denounced. Even those who disagreed with the killing of Riggs could not help also disagreeing with the killing of people being held in custody. *El Imparcial* stressed the nationalists' right to a trial and *El Mundo* denounced the abuse of power. Thousands of people were reported at their funeral service.[33] At the service, Don Pedro defiantly said:

> *"These two brave men who lie here tell us that the oath in Puerto Rico is valid and sealed with immortal blood. They will be able to kill 10,000 nationalists, but that is nothing because a million Puerto Ricans will emerge."*

Many also saw the avenging of the victims of the Río Piedras Massacre as a heroic act. In fact, there was considerable demand for the picture of Elías Beauchamp rendering a military salute taken by a photographer from *El Imparcial* just before he was brought into the police station. This picture was displayed inside many homes and Puerto Ricans wrote to *El Imparcial* requesting copies of the image so much that a notice was included in the paper informing readers their requests had been received and that they could obtain copies of the photo by visiting their office.

Seditious Conspiracy And The Tydings Bill

In the aftermath of the killing of Chief of Police Riggs, the residences and offices of Nationalist Party members were raided and, in addition to being

Fotografías de Elías Beauchamp

A todas las personas que nos han solicitado copias, de la fotografía de Elías Beauchamp, les advertimos que ya están a su disposición y que pueden pasar a recogerlas en nuestra Administración.

El Imparcial, 27 Feb 1936 (Historical Journals and Periodicals, Center for Puerto Rican Studies Library and Archives (Hunter College, CUNY))

arrested, some nationalists even disappeared without being heard from again. On March 5, 1936 the U.S. District Court in Puerto Rico ordered the arrest of Don Pedro under the charge of seditious conspiracy— "conspiring to overthrow the government of the United States in Puerto Rico." Then, on April 3, a Federal Grand Jury found probable cause to prosecute Don Pedro and eight other nationalists.[34] After paying the necessary costs, Don Pedro remained out on bail pending trial by jury.

A close friend of Riggs, Senator Millard Tydings (Maryland-D), retaliated for the death of his close friend in his own way when, on April 23, 1936, he introduced a bill in the Senate that allowed for Puerto Rico's independence. According to a correspondent for *La Democracia* working in Washington, the bill was drafted "within a spirit of vengeance against Puerto Ricans, offering the option of the present colonial formula or independence with

El Imparcial, 24 Feb 1936 (Historical Journals and Periodicals, Center for Puerto Rican Studies Library and Archives (Hunter College, CUNY))

starvation." If passed, it would result in a November 1937 plebiscite where Puerto Ricans were to vote 'yes' or 'no' for independence. In the case a majority voted 'yes,' then Puerto Rico would become independent in four years with each year seeing the tariff costs of Puerto Rican products increased by 25%.

The bill caused a great stir among Puerto Rico's politicians, but not in the way U.S. officials might have anticipated or hoped. Interestingly, despite its guarantee of economic and social ruin, leaders began to discuss the bill's offer of independence. Pro-statehood leader Rafael Martínez Nadal even said that, if the bill gets passed, "all men who feel free must vote for the Puerto Rican Republic." Don Pedro, out on bail awaiting trial, seized the moment and made a call for the leaders of Puerto Rico to immediately hold a constitutional convention.[35]

What followed was the development of a broad movement in support of declaring Puerto Rico's immediate independence. Completely downplaying its enormous historical significance, this movement that formed has been overshadowed by the political trial Don Pedro was subjected to, if not omitted outright, in every popular historical account of him during this period.

Chapter 20: Months From Independence

The Widespread Movement For A Constitutional Convention

Though the Tydings Bill had serious and decidedly harmful design flaws, when it was introduced on April 23, 1936, a nation-wide conversation on independence began. Even Rafael Martínez Nadal, the pro-statehood leader of the *Partido Unión Republicana*, was quoted in *El Mundo* on April 25 saying "Rather than lifelong slaves, rather than think of the political slavery of our children and grandchildren, our choice is not in doubt. Any man worthy of being called a son of this land, rather than ignominy with a full stomach, must prefer hunger with dignity and honor... every man who feels himself to be free must vote for the Republic of Puerto Rico."

Antonio Romero Barceló, leader of the *Partido Liberal de Puerto Rico*, was also quoted saying, "If circumstances come to put us in a situation without alternatives, we are resolutely bound to demand the independence of the homeland... even if we starve to death."

Also on April 25, the mayor of Aguas Buenas, where Don Pedro was living at the time, hosted a meeting with the local leaders of Puerto Rico's three main political parties—the Liberal Party, Socialist Party, and Republican Union. This meeting resulted in a call to the presidents of those parties, and Don Pedro, to immediately hold the constitutional convention to establish the Republic of Puerto Rico. The call was responded to favorably by those party's presidents and enthusiastically echoed by their local political leaders, student leaders, and other organizational leaders throughout Puerto Rico.

On May 4, several hundred people, including intellectuals and representatives from civil, social, and cultural groups, held an assembly in the *Ateneo Puertorriqueño* and formed the *Frente Unido por la Constitución de la República*. This broad front regularly engaged leaders from all of Puerto Rico's political parties in addition to other groups and organizations. Their first major public event took place May 10 in Caguas and had about 10,000 people in attendance with some 350,000 more estimated as listening to its radio broadcast. The newspaper *El Imparcial* regularly published an "honor roll" of municipalities where the U.S. flag was lowered, and the Puerto Rican flag raised in City Hall in support of the constitutional convention movement. By May 12, *El Imparcial* listed thirty municipalities. More towns eventually joined.

Cuadro de Honor

De los Ayuntamientos que han Izado los Colores Patrios

El siguiente cuadro de honor muestra, en orden alfabético, la lista de municipios en cuyas astas ha ondeado ya la bandera gloriosa de Puerto Rico: nuestro símbolo supremo:

AGUAS BUENAS, AGUADA, AIBONITO, ARROYO, CAYEY, CAGUAS, GURABO, CIDRA, JAYUYA, LARES, MARICAO, MAYAGUEZ, NARANJITO, OROCOVIS, PONCE, RINCON, TRUJILLO ALTO, TOA ALTA, UTUADO, VEGA ALTA, SAN GERMAN, ARECIBO, CAMUY, COROZAL, CABO ROJO, SABANA GRANDE, MOCA, COAMO, HATILLO, YABUCOA.

El Imparcial, 12 May 1936 (Historical Journals and Periodicals, Center for Puerto Rican Studies Library and Archives (Hunter College, CUNY))

Besides the more than thirty town halls previously mentioned, the Puerto Rican flag was also raised outside of the University of Puerto Rico, several high schools, and other prominent locations by people of all ages, but especially young people. These occurrences were widely publicized in newspapers, sometimes daily. One such occurrence at Santurce's Central High School, on May 12, received front page coverage. As students protested under the raised flag of Puerto Rico, police appeared and drew their guns as the students became more energized. Negotiating and getting the police to withdraw, the students then began to riot, destroying the inside of Central High. When the police arrived again, they clubbed the students, used tear gas, and fired shots in the air until the rioting ended. With the students continuing to demonstrate, Governor Winship then mobilized two National Guard units to intervene.

Don Pedro And The Constitutional Convention

When Don Pedro began the push for a constitutional convention it was significant because of both its timing and the level of thought he had put into it. His thoughts on the topic had been published in the media since at least 1923 without grabbing much attention or support. In this environment following the introduction of the Tydings Bill, *El Mundo* began to publish four newly written articles by Don Pedro on the constitutional convention.[36]

These articles, between April 27 and May 28, covered topics that included: the process for organizing a constitutional convention in Puerto Rico; similar conventions held in Cuba and the Dominican Republic that the U.S. took part in; the ruinous relationship the U.S. has had with Puerto Rico; the importance of the convention in organizing a legitimate power in Puerto Rico and electing its legitimate representatives; and, as time passed, the inability of Puerto Rico's political leaders to actually come together.

The purpose of the constitutional convention was two-fold: 1) to establish the sovereign power of Puerto Rico as a free nation; and 2) to elect the legitimate representatives of Puerto Rico that would negotiate a treaty with the United States. According to Don Pedro:

> *"[The existing political parties] do not represent the legitimate national will, owing to the conflict of interests between them. Partisanship can end only in a Constitutional Convention that also solemnly invests in its plenipotentiaries the power of the homeland."*

He then wrote:

> *"After the Constitutional Convention meets and the respective plenipotentiaries are designated, then we can do all the studies necessary to determine the international relations between the United States and Puerto Rico through the respective treaty; all the time can be taken that is necessary to resolve a matter so vital; but this time will be spent by people with the power to resolve it."*

For Don Pedro, the constitutional convention was the only diplomatic way out of Puerto Rico's colonial condition. Through it, legitimate representatives would be democratically chosen to negotiate a treaty, as equals, with the United States who, in turn, must offer due respect to these representatives, chosen as they were through a legitimate process involving honest and energetic national dialogue.

The idea of a plebiscite was criticized by Don Pedro as both inappropriate and offensive. He explained in an interview published on May 2:

> *"First of all, the plebiscite is a legislative formula that is used to consult the will of the inhabitants who occupy a strip of land between two sovereign nations when the population of the two sovereigns has been mixed in such a way that it is not possible to draw a territorial limit to divide them; the Plebiscite is never used to consult the national will of a duly constituted nation to ask whether it wants to be free."*

As far as what this constitutional convention process would look like, Don Pedro offered the following outline:

"Each political party can hold a national convention and designate the number of delegates that have the right to represent them in the Constitutional Convention according to the prior agreement arrived at by all the political parties. These conventions of the respective political parties can be held the same day, and on the next the Constitutional Convention can be held with the designated delegations of the respective political parties. This Constitutional Convention can then designate the plenipotentiaries of Puerto Rico in order to resolve with plenipotentiaries of the United States everything concerning a permanent treaty between both nations."

The Empire Intervenes

While Don Pedro's push for a constitutional convention received much more support than in the past, the colonial regime inevitably worked against and prevented it from taking place. First, Governor Winship began prohibiting public meetings at the onset of the movement, leading to increased repression by police. Second, the approaching November elections began to take the focus of the political leaders. Third, political leaders, especially Luis Muñoz Marín, who spent much of his time during this period in Washington, began to engage in negotiations over the terms of the Tydings Bill and what independence could look like.[37]

Regarding the third aspect, Don Pedro was very clear in his critique of politicians negotiating with U.S. officials around independence. Essentially calling out what he saw as the backwards nature of these negotiations, he said, "They are beginning where they should end, and they want to end where they should begin." In other words, instead of discussing the terms of independence with U.S. officials before exercising their sovereignty, Puerto Rico's political leaders should be exercising their sovereignty through the constitutional convention process and then discussing after that the terms of the international relations between the Republic of Puerto Rico and the United States government.

The attention given to Don Pedro and the Nationalist Party by the colonial regime was significant in this period. On May 7, Colonel Cole wrote a report speaking to the threat they posed during the campaign for a constitutional convention. In the report, he said that if independence was given to Puerto Rico, the environment "will give Albizu Campos more than a fair chance of becoming the head of government." Reports from the U.S. Army's Military Intelligence Division during July and August also show the close attention the regime was paying to the trial of Don Pedro and other Party members.[38]

The conviction of Don Pedro for seditious conspiracy in the moment he is receiving considerable support for holding a constitutional convention is no coincidence. A national process beginning with an assertion of sovereignty and involving a later treaty negotiation to end the U.S. occupation of Puerto Rico was obviously a scenario the colonial power structure wanted to avoid. When visited by his wife in jail after his July 31 sentencing, and before being sent to Atlanta Penitentiary, Don Pedro said the U.S. knew exactly what they had in their hands: "if they had left me six more months in the streets, I would have made the Republic."[39]

The 1936 movement for a constitutional convention led by Don Pedro is a significant event in the history of Puerto Rico's struggle for independence. Unfortunately, the movement has been overshadowed in historical texts by the trial of Don Pedro and the Nationalist Party members, if it is mentioned at all. The push for a constitutional convention was an incredible expression of Don Pedro's nationalist philosophy in its most diplomatic sense. It embodies three key aspects of Don Pedro's nationalist philosophy: the nullity of the Treaty of Paris, the boycott of elections, and non-recognition of the authority of the U.S. regime. While his imprisonment was itself significant, the pro-convention movement adds a whole other contextual understanding to it that can inform a re-interpretation of this period in his leadership.

Chapter 21: Prison And The Ponce Massacre

Imprisoning National Leadership

By the time Don Pedro and the eight other Nationalist Party members were indicted on April 3, 1936, for seditious conspiracy and other charges, one of the accused—Juan Antonio Corretjer—had already begun serving a one-year sentence for contempt. Ordered by a Federal Grand Jury subpoena to produce four years' worth of internal Party documents, Corretjer, as secretary general of the Party, refused to comply. Commenting on the issuing of the subpoena to hand over internal documents, Don Pedro said:

> *"It is a process in which the accused are to provide the evidence that the prosecutor needs, which is demonstrative that there is no evidence. In other words, it is an unusual process in which the defendants are required to provide evidence for their own conviction, which is contrary to all principles of law."*

When the trial finally got underway, the jury was composed of six Puerto Ricans and five Americans. On July 19 the jury did not arrive at an agreement, with the six Puerto Ricans each calling for an acquittal on all charges, and the five Americans calling for a guilty verdict on all charges. This resulted in Judge Robert Cooper dissolving the jury and calling for the formation of a second jury.

The second jury was composed of ten Americans and two Puerto Ricans with strong ties to American corporations. According to American painter Rockwell Kent, the prosecutor Cecil Snyder showed a list of names to a friend at a party just after the first trial. Snyder claimed they were the names of the jurors for the second trial, implying that they had essentially been hand-picked. These jurors, on July 31, arrived at guilty verdicts for all the accused.[40]

One juror, Elmer Ellsworth, later testified that Judge Cooper influenced him into voting guilty, also saying that "It was evident from the composition of the jury that the nationalists did not and could not have a fair trial." The trial was a scene of colonial intimidation, with police lined up outside the courthouse with machine guns, rifles, and gas grenades, accompanied by both the chief of police and commander of the U.S. Army in Puerto Rico.

As soon as charges were made, one of the accused nationalists, Rafael Ortiz Pacheco, escaped to the Dominican Republic without notifying his comrades. Following the verdict of July 31, 1936, Don Pedro and the other nationalists were taken to *La Princesa* jail in San Juan while an appeal was made on their behalf. They stayed there until finally transferred to Atlanta Penitentiary on June 7, 1937. Don Pedro was sentenced to six years in prison followed by an additional four years on probation.[41]

All the nationalists sentenced to imprisonment were prominent leaders of the Party and their exile was a serious blow to the nationalist movement.

The Ponce Massacre

After their conviction, the nationalists were held in *La Princesa* during the appeals process. The Nationalist Party remained active. For Sunday, March 21, 1937, the Party organized a march in Ponce to commemorate the abolition of slavery in Puerto Rico, which took effect on March 22, 1873. The day's activities were to end with a protest of the incarceration of their leaders. Visited by the new chief of police just before starting, the gathered nationalists were told the mayor of Ponce had suddenly revoked the authorization he had given prior for the event. Asserting their right to freedom of expression, the Cadets and Nurses of the Liberation Army defied the revocation and proceeded as planned.

With a few hundred people gathered, the nationalists fell into military formation in the middle of the street. As armed policemen situated themselves in the four streets surrounding the unarmed protestors, a band began to play the music for La Borinqueña. Immediately responding to this cue, the leader of the Cadets, Tomás López de Victoria, ordered the formation to begin marching.

Almost instantaneously, the police began shooting on the crowd from all angles. In the ensuing chaos, nineteen people were killed, with another 150-200 being wounded. The event became known as the Ponce Massacre. The nineteen victims killed by police included men, women, and children, the youngest being seven years old. Both nationalists and non-nationalists were killed, in addition to two policemen killed by friendly fire.[42]

The American Civil Liberties Union (ACLU) created a commission to investigate the event. Headed by Arthur Garfield Hays, the ACLU's president, the commission also included various Puerto Ricans of well-respected institutions such as the *Ateneo Puertorriqueño*, the Bar Association, the Teachers Association, the Medical Association, and various national newspapers. The commission concluded that the event was indeed a "massacre," and that it was the result of the denial by police of the right to assembly on orders of Governor Winship. It also highlighted the fact that Governor Winship, in the months prior, had a clear practice of denying Puerto Ricans their right to free speech and assembly and having them arrested when exercising those rights.

In his book *War Against All Puerto Ricans*, author Nelson A. Denis points out that eleven of the fourteen articles in 1937 covering the Ponce Massacre in the New York Times used the word "riot" to describe the event. Incredibly, twenty-three nationalists present that day received charges, eleven with murder to be tried by a jury. On February 1, 1938, this trial resulted in all of the nationalists being acquitted. No police were ever held responsible.

The Inspiration Of Don Pedro

One of the most tragic events in Puerto Rican history, a focus on the actions taken by nationalists reveals a militant and deep commitment to Puerto Rico's liberation. They also point to the profound influence Don Pedro had on the character of Party members regarding the honoring of national symbols and developing a spirit of *valor y sacrificio.*

One of the traditions started by Don Pedro that was present at the event led by nationalists that day was the singing of La Borinqueña, the revolutionary anthem of Puerto Rico. It was to this tune that the Cadets and Nurses of the Liberation Army marched, accompanied by the public in attendance.

Tomás López de Victoria, the commander of the Ponce section of the Liberation Army, maintained a militant discipline and defied the presence of armed police by giving the order to march once La Borinqueña began. This decision, considering the recent killing and jailing of nationalists, was a clear display of courage and sacrifice.

At one point during those nearly twenty minutes when the police were beating protestors with clubs and shooting them with machine guns, even those with raised hands, the Puerto Rican flag fell to the ground. Noticing this while running for cover, a black woman and nationalist who traveled to the protest from Mayagüez, Dominga de la Cruz Becerril, turned around and ran through the massacre to pick the flag up, only then running to find cover. When asked why she did this, she explained that Don Pedro had said "the flag should never touch the ground."[43]

In these moments, a cadet shot by police named Bolívar Márquez Telechea was also bleeding to death. Before dying, his last act of nationalist defiance was to write "*¡Que Viva la República, Abajo los Asesinos!*"[44] with three crosses in his own blood on the nearest wall.[45]

Notes To Chapters 13 - 21

[1] Corretjer, *La Lucha por la Independencia de Puerto Rico.*

[2] Torres, ed., *Obras Escogidas, Tomo I.*

[3] These elections take place every four years.

[4] Rosado, *Las Llamas de la Aurora.*

[5] The electoral boycott, as a form of resistance, was known as retraimiento.

[6] Rosado, *Las Llamas de la Aurora.*

[7] The New York Times, *Dr. Rhoads Cleared of Porto Rico Plot.*

[8] IPS Correspondents, *Group Strips Racist Scientist's Name from Award.*

[9] The New York Times, *Mob Invades New Capitol of Porto Rico.*

[10] The New York Times, *Albizu and Portilla Are Freed of Capitol Riot Charge.*

[11] Torres, ed., *Obras Escogidas, Tomo I.*

[12] Medina Ramírez, *El Movimiento Libertador en la Historia de Puerto Rico.*

[13] Rosado, *Las Llamas de la Aurora.*

[14] This case was known as "Velázquez' Slap in the Face." The day after participating in an event honoring the U.S. flag on June 14, 1932, the chief justice of the Puerto Rican Supreme Court, Emilio del Toro y Cuebas, was visited in his office by Velázquez who, after stating his actions "constituted an open defiance to our homeland," slapped him across the face. Velázquez was charged with assault and convicted in Municipal Court. After an appeals process, the conviction was overturned because the assault took place in a building under U.S. government jurisdiction and thus could not be tried in a municipal court.

[15] Torres, ed., *Obras Escogidas, Tomo I.*

[16] Torres, ed., *Obras Escogidas, Tomo II.*

[17] For more on Don Pedro Angleró and his passing, see Chapter 37.

[18] Torres, ed., *Obras Escogidas, Tomo I.*

[19] Silén, *Pedro Albizu Campos y el Nacionalismo Irlandés.*

[20] These 33 were: Gurabo, Vieques, Guayama, Arroyo, Patillas, Barranquitas, Aguadilla, Aguada, Rincón, Isabela, Lares, Arecibo, Utuado, Barceloneta, San Juan, Bayamón, Dorado, Vega Baja, Comerio, Vega Alta, Toa Baja, Cataño, Humacao, Yabucoa, Naguabo, Maunabo, Fajardo, Mayagüez, Lajas, Añasco, Cabo Rojo, Sabana Grande, San Germán.

[21] Denis, *War Against All Puerto Ricans.*

[22] One flag is associated with El Grito de Lares, and the other was adopted in 1895 New York City by the Revolutionary Committee of Puerto Rico, a chapter of the Cuban Revolutionary Party.

[23] Dávila, *de las Hijas de la Libertad al Cuerpo de Enfermeras de la República del Partido Nacionalista de Puerto Rico.*

[24] Rosado, *Las Llamas de la Aurora.*

[25] Laura de Albizu Campos, *Albizu Campos y la Independencia de Puerto Rico.*

[26] Rosado, *Las Llamas de la Aurora.*

[27] Denis, *War Against All Puerto Ricans.*

[28] Corretjer, *La Lucha por la Independencia de Puerto Rico.*

[29] Rosado, *El Nacionalismo y la Violencia en la Década de 1930.*

[30] Rosado, *Las Llamas de la Aurora.*

[31] Denis, *War Against All Puerto Ricans.* Torres, ed., *Obras Escogidas, Tomo II.*

[32] Corretjer, *La Lucha por la Independencia de Puerto Rico.*

[33] Rosado, *El Nacionalismo y la Violencia en la Década de 1930.*

[34] The other eight nationalists were Juan Antonio Corretjer, Luis F. Velázquez, Clemente Soto Vélez, Erasmo Velázquez, Julio H. Velázquez, Juan Gallardo Santiago, Juan Juarbe Juarbe, and Pablo Rosado Ortiz.

[35] Torres, ed., *Obras Escogidas, Tomo III.*

[36] Torres, ed., *Obras Escogidas, Tomo III.*

[37] Rosado, *Las Llamas de la Aurora.*

[38] Estades-Font, *The Critical Year of 1936 through the Reports of the Military Intelligence Division.*

[39] Laura de Albizu Campos, *Albizu Campos y la Independencia de Puerto Rico.*

[40] Denis, *War Against All Puerto Ricans.*

41 Torres, *El Proceso Judicial Contra Pedro Albizu Campos En El 1936.*

42 Rosado, *El Nacionalismo y la Violencia en la Década de 1930.*

43 Jiménez de Wagenheim, *Nationalist Heroines.*

44 Long live the Republic, Down with the murderers.

45 Rosado, *Las Llamas de la Aurora.*

Fifth Period — 10 Years Of Exile

Chapter 22: Atlanta Penitentiary

Life In Atlanta Penitentiary

Don Pedro and the seven other convicted nationalists were transferred to Atlanta Penitentiary on June 7, 1937. When they arrived, they were assigned a number that guards and prison officials used to address them from that point on. Don Pedro was '51298.' At the time, the prison housed around 3,000 convicted persons and was located on an area made up of three hundred acres.[1]

An agent performing an investigation requested by prosecutor Cecil Snyder recommended Don Pedro not be sent to Atlanta Penitentiary, "since he was the only one in the group that was not white and in those prisons he would 'certainly' be the victim of racism by the officers in charge of the prisoners, most of which came from 'southern states.'"

Interestingly, while the prison did separate black people convicted of crimes from the rest of the population, Don Pedro was kept with the general population. On his in-processing papers, Don Pedro was described as "a somewhat sparsely built young white man, of middle aged, who is married and the father of three children."

The typical day started with a 6AM wake-up. A small breakfast was served an hour and a half later. Mandated to have and maintain a job, by 7:45AM the people that were incarcerated had to be ready to perform their job duties. Stopping work at 11AM, they had some time to rest and then were served lunch. At 1PM they resumed work for two hours and then were given one hour for recreation. 4:30PM was dinner time. During the summer, recreation was extended until 6:30PM when the people incarcerated were locked into their cells for the night. Lights out was at 9PM. They were allowed to bathe only twice a week, did not work on the weekends, and had a radio in their cell that went off with the lights at night.

The people incarcerated at Atlanta Penitentiary were allowed to receive mail, but Don Pedro was given special treatment—he could not receive magazines or newspapers, was only allowed to correspond with an authorized list of people, had to have all correspondence written in English, and all his mail was opened and inspected by officials who then decided whether to deliver or keep them. The other nationalists, who were all separated from each other, for the most part had the same conditions. Since most of them did not know English, they were allowed to receive letters in Spanish, but Don Pedro first had to translate them for prison officials.

Regarding visits, Don Pedro was allowed one per month. Sometimes, as happened to Chilean poet and future Nobel Prize in Literature winner Gabriela Mistral, his visitors were turned away.[2] East Harlem Congressman Vito Marcantonio is said to have visited him five times.

Don Pedro's Activities

During the period when he was in Atlanta Penitentiary, Don Pedro initially worked as a janitor but was then transferred to the prison library when his level of education became apparent to prison officials. At some point, he worked as a proofreader that corrected all the work other incarcerated people completed in the prison's educational program, which was mandated for everyone. Don Pedro also led classes in Catholicism. Due to the positive reputation he had, Don Pedro influenced many of his students to attend mass every Sunday and on holy days. A 'Parole Progress Report' of May 29, 1939 stated, "He is truly trying to live a good Christian life."

In addition to the letters he wrote to family and other authorized persons, and despite the restrictions placed upon mail, Don Pedro is said to have managed to write and send out articles that were published in Mexico and Buenos Aires under the pseudonym Pedro Gringoire. The article attributed to him in Mexico, titled 'Puerto Rico Aspires To Its Freedom,' was published in *Magazín Excelsior*.

In Buenos Aires, two of his articles were published in *Claridad* magazine, one titled 'El Nacionalismo Borinqueño,' and another titled 'The Recognition of the Independence of Puerto Rico Is An Irrevocable Imperative.' One topic discussed in the articles was the Liberation Army and the struggle's need for arms:

> *"The cadets of the Republic are today, perhaps, the most glorious army in the world. They are at least the only legitimate military organization in Puerto Rico, because their authority does not stem from a usurpation but from a right. They have marched unarmed in front of the enemy's guns and will march armed along the enemy's fortified line. Nationalism needs weapons, weapons, weapons. It needs guns, rifles, machine guns…"*

Another topic was their struggle in relation to the people of the U.S.:

> *"We can say without any false sense of pride that the only one in Puerto Rico that has a true concept of friendship and understanding towards the United States is the Nationalist Party. Our complaint is not against the American people, because the American people are not to blame for what is happening in Puerto Rico."*

During Don Pedro's exile, the Nationalist Party continued to elect him as their president. They also elected an interim president. Don Pedro's status as the central leader of the Nationalist Party allowed him to continue influencing its direction. For example, just before the United States' entry into World War 2, Don Pedro put out a directive, which was approved, that called on all Party members to refuse being drafted into the U.S. Armed Forces. This decision resulted in the jailing of about 50 nationalists from 1940-1944.

Don Pedro's Health

It is clear that the conditions Don Pedro faced in prison seriously affected his health, even before he left for Atlanta Penitentiary. According to an interview with Rafael Raldiris, a formerly incarcerated person in Atlanta Penitentiary who returned to Puerto Rico after completing his sentence, Don Pedro arrived in prison already sick and was put under treatment for anemia. In August 1937 he experienced a 35% level of hemoglobin and was hospitalized in September due to a suspected case of tuberculosis, which a chest x-ray ruled out. His hemoglobin levels did not stabilize until May 1939 when their levels were measured at 82%.[3]

Fellow nationalist in prison Clemente Soto Vélez said the following about Don Pedro's health: "There was a time when he and I both thought that the leader would not survive the state of health that forced the administration to hospitalize him in the prison itself."

The care eventually given to Don Pedro, which was less than adequate, came only as a result of complaints made by Congressman Vito Marcantonio. Writing the attorney general, the surgeon general, and the medical officer of Atlanta Penitentiary, Marcantonio also requested that a specific doctor be able to examine Don Pedro. His request was denied. Following a visit to the prison by Andrew Newhoff of the Committee for Political Prisoners, an article in *Diario La Correspondencia de Puerto Rico* repeated Newhoff's urging to provide Don Pedro medical attention. Newhoff highlighted his "serious" and "unfortunate state of health."

The book *Albizu Campos: Preso En Atlanta*, edited by Carmelo Rosario Natal, provides insight into the consistent work of the American Civil Liberties Union (ACLU) in not only advocating for the release of the nationalists in prison but for applying pressure so that Don Pedro could receive much-needed medical attention.[4]

The book also shows how the ACLU communicated closely with Don Pedro's wife, Doña Laura, to exchange information and coordinate efforts related to his condition. Doña Laura worked from within Latin America in their efforts to secure medical attention for Don Pedro. Speaking to the mental exhaustion induced upon him as a result of constant health battles, Clemente Soto Vélez described how "Albizu's precarious health was another constant torture to his conscience."

Chapter 23: The Campaign To Free The Nationalists

Immediate Support For The Nationalists

Before Don Pedro and the seven other Nationalist Party members were sentenced to prison, they were already receiving significant support. Many people even sacrificed their own personal funds to contribute to the costs of their legal defense. Immediately after their trial ended, a meeting was held on August 9, 1936 in San Juan's Municipal Theater. In this meeting the National Congress for the Freedom of the Political Prisoners was organized. This National Congress worked on a continental level to gain support for the release of the nationalists. The more than twenty thousand dollars they raised were used for court proceedings and to maintain a group of delegates throughout Latin America.

President Franklin D. Roosevelt received numerous appeals for the commutation of the sentences of the nationalists. On September 15, 1936, one appeal was signed by intellectuals from France, Belgium, Colombia, Italy, Egypt, Switzerland, Catalonia, Palestine, Brazil, Spain, Uruguay, Australia, Bolivia, Argentina, and the Dominican Republic. On another, 100 prominent intellectuals and leaders in the U.S. wrote the president, including Ernest Hemingway, Langston Hughes, Sherwood Anderson, Ruth Benedict, and Adam Clayton Powell, Jr., among others.[5]

Luz María Serradel, a friend of Don Pedro's from Harvard, wrote a letter to President Roosevelt with a list of signatures from members of the Mexican Committee For The Freedom Of Pedro Albizu Campos.

Henry Epstein, who also knew Don Pedro at Harvard and was serving as the New York State attorney general, also wrote a letter to President Roosevelt asking for his release.

Several international congresses also joined in calling for the release of the nationalists. At the Inter-American Conference for the Maintenance of Peace, held in Buenos Aires in December 1936, Don Pedro was declared "Hero of America" and "Moral President of the Anti-Imperialist Consciousness of the entire Continent."[6]

A week before the Conference opened, a letter signed by the Executive Committee of the National Clergy of Puerto Rico was sent to the president of Argentina. In this letter they wrote, "The invading intervention has culminated with a policy of terrorism that has been unraveled against the nation's purest leadership." They also explained that, in their view, the nationalists' only charge was "defending the independence of our land."[7]

East Harlem Congressman Vito Marcantonio

One individual deserving of separate mention that was active in the campaign to free Don Pedro and the nationalists was Vito Marcantonio. An Italian American politician born, raised, and a permanent resident of East Harlem, Marcantonio was a New York University-trained lawyer able to secure overwhelming support from the constituents in his district and a seat in Congress for more than a decade. This support was earned not only by his radical, people-centered politics, but also by the practical services thousands of his constituents received through his volunteers.[8]

Due to the large Puerto Rican population of East Harlem, Vito Marcantonio became known as a defender of Puerto Rican rights. Becoming an ally of the Nationalist Party, which had a very active chapter in New York, he was able to use his place within Congress in their favor. This contrasted with Puerto Rico's resident commissioner in Congress who is a non-voting member. When the Tydings Bill was introduced in 1936, Marcantonio responded with a bill of his own, saying, "Genuine independence and the declaration of the responsibility of the United States for the present disastrous state of the economy of Puerto Rico and the abysmal poverty of its people, is the purpose of my bill."[9]

Following the indictment of the nationalists for seditious conspiracy, Marcantonio took an active interest in their defense. Invited by the defense to become part of their team, he wrote Judge Cooper asking the trial be delayed a few days so he could travel to Puerto Rico and be present for it. This request was denied. The reason for his denial was an effort by U.S. authorities to prevent him from arriving on time, which Pan American Airways assisted by denying him flights for over a week.

Marcantonio was known for traveling almost exclusively between New York's City Hall, his congressional district, and Washington, D.C., and for spending the great majority of his time in East Harlem. When Marcantonio finally landed in Puerto Rico on August 1, 1936, it became his first and only time outside of the continental U.S. Almost immediately, Marcantonio was joined by members of the defense in a visit to Don Pedro in jail.

Marcantonio had his first opportunity to speak in court following a petition for a new trial filed August 3rd. Marcantonio's main argument in court was the existence of evidence showing three jurors held a bias against Don Pedro and the nationalists. While in Puerto Rico he also had a meeting with Ernest Gruening, Director of the Division of Territories and Island Possessions of the U.S. Department of the Interior. In this meeting he unsuccessfully tried to gain Gruening's support for the nationalists' release.

When Marcantonio returned to New York on August 11 he began working to mobilize stateside support for the nationalists. This effort resulted in the formation of the American Committee for the Defense of Puerto Rican

Political Prisoners, an organization composed of elements from some thirty organizations. Marcantonio would continue his efforts to expose the bias of the jurors and the political nature of the trial.

Vito Marcantonio

Continued Support For The Exiled

In 1937, four prominent international congresses were held that included among their activities a call for the release of the nationalists: the Pan-American Press Conference held in Chile, the World Youth Congress held in New York's Vassar College, and two other congresses held in Mexico. In October 1938, the Pan-American Colombian Society approved a resolution to begin a continental campaign for the release of the nationalists.

In March 1939, the Cuban Committee for the Freedom of the Puerto Rican Patriots was founded by faculty members of the University of Havana, Cuban students, lawyers, scientists, historians, journalists, writers, artists, and others.

Biographer Marisa Rosado lists several national and international bodies that called for the release of the nationalists, including the Popular Congress for American Peace in Buenos Aires, the Congress of Latin American Journalists in Valparaiso, Chile, the P.E.N. Club in Buenos Aires, the Senates of the Dominican Republic and Argentina, the Workers Congress of Guadalajara, Mexico, and the Constitutional Assembly of Cuba. She also lists several Cuban organizations, such as the Reporters Association of Havana, the Athens Club, the José Martí Popular University, the Revolutionary Union Party, the Union of Writers and Artists, the National Women's Union, the Anti-Imperialist Agrarian Youth, the Workers Confederation of Cuba, and others.

Many of these organizations wrote directly to the U.S. president calling for the release of the nationalists in prison. In the end, as Marisa Rosado writes, "All of these claims were ignored. It was obvious the United States authorities and their colonial associates wanted Albizu and the other nationalist leaders in jail. The republic, another Latin American republic, was not what they wanted as a system of government in Puerto Rico." Clearly, with all the support the nationalists received, from so many countries, from prominent individuals spanning countless segments of American and international society, and from politicians in their very House of Representatives, the United States meant to keep them in jail in order to crush the movement for independence.

Chapter 24: Columbus Hospital

Leaving Atlanta Penitentiary For New York

Don Pedro became eligible for parole in 1941. An FBI document details his response: "On November 4, 1941, he was eligible for conditional release but refused to execute the necessary conditional release papers on the grounds that by doing so he would be recognizing the United States Government, and, in view of his Nationalist beliefs, he could not acquiesce to these regulatory terms." Don Pedro remained in Atlanta Penitentiary until being released on June 3, 1943. Refusing to recognize the authority of the U.S. government over him, he made it clear that once released he would consider himself free beyond any condition. Don Pedro also made it clear that he would not write to Judge Cooper requesting permission to stay in New York to complete the final part of his sentence, or declare his residence each month to U.S. officials, as was requested of him.

Clemente Soto Vélez, Luis F. Velázquez, and Juan Antonio Corretjer had moved to New York once they were released and played a role in the organizational efforts of the Nationalist Party's chapter there. Well-organized during this time period, the New York chapter had opened three social-cultural clubs—one each in Manhattan, Brooklyn, and the Bronx—whose fundraising efforts helped the Party economically.[10]

When Don Pedro was released from Atlanta penitentiary, this New York chapter of the Nationalist Party sent Corretjer and fellow nationalist Julio Pinto Gandía to serve as escorts to New York. Vito Marcantonio also sent a lawyer, Samuel Newberger, to accompany Don Pedro on the trip and provide legal assistance if needed. They rode a train to New York in a private car of the train paid for by the Communist Party, USA.

When Don Pedro left Atlanta Penitentiary his health was still problematic. Just three days after leaving prison he was admitted into Columbus Hospital on 19th Street between Second and Third Avenue. At admission, Don Pedro had symptoms including shortness of breath, tightness and pain in his chest, swollen glands in his groin, swollen legs, a feeling of paralysis on the left side of his body, and insomnia. His diagnosis was arteriosclerosis, coronary sclerosis, bronchial neuritis, and general weakness. Don Pedro's attending physician that Vito Marcantonio arranged to care for him, Dr. Epaminondas Secondary, was a heart disease specialist trained in Austria said to be a refugee from Mussolini's Italy.

Two Years Of Recovery And Surveillance

For two years, Don Pedro remained in Columbus Hospital as a patient. Despite the genuinely poor state of his health, Don Pedro's long-term stay at Columbus Hospital was the subject of criticism by federal authorities. Director of the FBI J. Edgar Hoover, for example, said the following in a report: "Albizu Campos is reported to be using his private room in the Columbus Hospital as the headquarters of the Nationalist Party of Puerto Rico in New York City and it has been said that he receives many notable visitors and holds meetings in this room, which, according to reliable sources, is paid for by the Communist Party, U.S.A.... Sources, who are deemed to be familiar with the instant matter, have indicated that it would appear that Albizu Campos continues to be hospitalized on his own volition in order to elicit sympathy from and appear as a martyr to the members and adherents of his party who are of the opinion that he was unjustly incarcerated in the Atlanta Penitentiary and that this imprisonment resulted in a breakdown of health."

Federal agents continued to conduct surveillance on Don Pedro while he was in Columbus Hospital. They were fully aware of the people that went to visit him and received further information from informants. Microphones were also placed in Don Pedro's hospital room and in one of his visits to see him, Vito Marcantonio discovered one of them. Marcantonio screamed obscenities into it, ripped it out of the wall, and threatened those who were listening to produce the microphone in a congressional meeting.

The persecution faced by Don Pedro, most immediately expressed as the surveillance conducted on him, became a concern. According to nationalist Gil Ramos Cancel, "his confinement in the Columbus Hospital was due to both health and safety reasons, to prevent him from being arrested for violation of the conditions imposed by his freedom, which he had not accepted or signed, but which were still in force."

When he left Columbus Hospital in November 1945, Don Pedro was in better physical condition but was documented as still suffering from arteriosclerosis. According to Ruth Reynolds, he should not have left the hospital but did so due to economic reasons.

Ruth Reynolds

Many people visited Don Pedro at Columbus Hospital. One of the people that spent a considerable amount of time with him was Ruth Reynolds. Very active around civil rights as a pacifist, Reynolds met nationalist leader Julio Pinto Gandía during a February 1944 demonstration in support of Mahatma Gandhi at the English Consulate. Told by Pinto Gandía that Puerto Rico's own leader of Gandhi-like status was in Columbus Hospital, she accepted an invitation to meet him.

Reynolds had heard of the Ponce Massacre but still had a hard time believing her own government was complicit in such an event. When she went to see Don Pedro, a survivor of the Ponce Massacre, Carmen

Fernández, happened to be present. After Don Pedro asked everyone to leave the room, Fernández took Reynolds to the bathroom and showed the bullet scars left on her body. Profoundly affected by what she saw, Reynolds from that day forward committed her life to the struggle for Puerto Rico's independence.[11]

In January of 1945, Reynolds helped to form the American League for the Independence of Puerto Rico, holding the position of secretary. The League took an active role in helping to bring awareness to Puerto Rico's struggle in significant ways.[12] In March, just two months after it was founded, they sent a letter to the U.S. secretary of state to point out the recent U.S. effort to prevent Julio Pinto Gandía from speaking as a representative of the Nationalist Party of Puerto Rico at the founding meeting of the United Nations in San Francisco. The letter emphasized the importance of working to accelerate legislation to secure Puerto Rico's independence.

In May 1947, Reynolds stood before the Subcommittee on Public Lands on the floor of the House of Representatives and spoke against a bill that would allow Puerto Ricans to elect their own governor without changing the colonial relationship. The ability of the League to engage North American activists and intellectuals through its numerous meetings and events around Puerto Rico's colonial case was significant.

In 1950, Reynolds was imprisoned in Puerto Rico following a revolt[13] organized by the Nationalist Party. She joined the more than one thousand people arrested in the days following the start of the revolt. Having spent a lot of time with Don Pedro in Columbus Hospital and becoming a close friend of his, Reynolds was able to learn a lot about his life and character.

Much of what she learned about him was later documented by the Center for Puerto Rican Studies (CENTRO) during over one hundred hours of interviews with Reynolds conducted by CENTRO staff member Blanca Vázquez from 1985 to 1986. This oral history, and the documents Reynolds donated, continues to be a notable resource for researchers of Don Pedro and the nationalist movement. A few years later, just months before her physical death in 1989, Hunter College published her account of the 1948 strike organized by students in the University of Puerto Rico that was also a protest against the colonial structure in Puerto Rico.

Under arrest in 1950, from r-l: Ruth Reynolds, Olga Viscal Garriga,
Carmen Maria Perez

Chapter 25: New York City

Don Pedro In New York City

While so much more can be written about Don Pedro's activities in New York City between the time he left Columbus Hospital and returned to Puerto Rico, the oral history of Ruth Reynolds provides several details.[14] As far as where he took up residence, Reynolds points to a few places, the first being an apartment in the South Bronx on 173 Brook Avenue where Oscar Collazo, a nationalist who later participated in an assassination attempt on President Truman, also lived. From there he moved to an apartment in El Barrio near Lexington Avenue and 114th Street that was rented by fellow nationalist leader Ramón Medina Ramírez.

Reynolds gives no indication why he moved from the South Bronx to El Barrio, but she does make very clear that any time Don Pedro was outside the island of Manhattan he was violating the terms of his parole that required him to remain there. After some time in El Barrio, Don Pedro had to move again because the schedule of one of Medina Ramírez' sons prevented him from getting proper rest. Making this move in the fall of 1946, Don Pedro went From El Barrio to an apartment in the Greenwich Village area.

After leaving Columbus Hospital, one consistent activity of Don Pedro was attending Catholic Mass on Sundays, apparently in La Milagrosa Church located on 114th Street and Seventh Avenue. He also enjoyed taking the Staten Island Ferry. The sea breezes not only reminded him of home, but they were supportive of his recovery. After these ferry rides, Reynolds said that she and Don Pedro sometimes grabbed food in Staten Island or during a quick stop in Brooklyn.

Another activity Don Pedro enjoyed was the occasional attendance of operas and ballets. For his protection, Don Pedro almost always had somebody with him, the exception being when he was living in the Village and walked to the home of Lolín Quintana who lived nearby on West 13th Street and 8th Avenue. At Quintana's house, Don Pedro received frequent visits on the weekends from various people. One of these visits is said to have been by members of the Irish Republican Army that he had known from his time in prison.

Don Pedro also oversaw a monthly publication run by Medina Ramírez, *La Revista de Puerto Rico*, even though he was not supposed to be politically active. Depending on his physical condition at the time, Don Pedro also accepted invitations to give lectures at cultural centers in the city. Clearly, while on parole

Don Pedro did hesitate to continue his political work in favor of Puerto Rico's independence. On one occasion, Don Pedro further tested the travel limitations placed upon him by crossing the border into Canada with Reynolds. The trip occurred without incident.

Remaining Committed To Puerto Rico

Despite spending so much time recovering in Columbus Hospital and living in exile in Manhattan, Don Pedro maintained influence over the Nationalist Party. From exile he continued to inform the direction of certain aspects of the Party. As evident in his work with Ruth Reynolds and the American League for Puerto Rico's Independence (ALPRI), Don Pedro ensured efforts were made to continue bringing international attention to Puerto Rico's colonial situation. A significant moment of this, which has been previously mentioned, took place in 1945 at the founding meeting of the United Nations (UN).

When the charter establishing the UN was created in 1945 San Francisco, the Nationalist Party had delegates present to observe the proceedings and network with the delegates present. The Party also put in an official request to be recognized as a non-governmental organization able to observe all future UN proceedings. This request was granted, and the Party chose Thelma Mielke, a North American pacifist/activist and member of ALPRI, as their permanent observer.

As the Nationalist Party took part in these UN meetings, they also shared with delegates from other countries information on Puerto Rico that was in contrast to the narrative put forth in the information given by U.S. officials. Don Pedro was updated on the proceedings of the UN while he was in New York. He saw the UN as an opportunity to reinvigorate international interest in and to gain support for Puerto Rico's anti-colonial struggle.

Don Pedro's absolute commitment to Puerto Rico was also shown in his resolve to return there once his parole was complete. This is especially evident when considering the offers for political asylum extended to him. Both Cuba and Mexico extended offers to reside in their countries instead of returning to Puerto Rico. They knew Don Pedro would most certainly be targeted again with every level of political repression. In a 1948 speech he spoke to the sense of duty he had in his commitment to Puerto Rico, declaring, "Albizu Campos has sworn that he will never lower his guard in defense of the freedom of his country."

On December 11, 1947, with his parole complete and the FBI still surveilling him, Don Pedro boarded a steamship in Brooklyn with a few compatriots. The steamship made it to port and Don Pedro finally returned to Puerto Rico following ten years of exile on December 15.[15]

Notes To Chapters 22 - 25

[1] Denis, *War Against All Puerto Ricans.*

[2] Laura de Albizu Campos, *Albizu Campos y la Independencia de Puerto Rico.*

[3] Rosado, *Las Llamas de la Aurora.*

[4] Rosario Natal, *Preso en Atlanta-Historia del Reo #51298-A (Correspondencia).*

[5] Rosado, *Las Llamas de la Aurora.*

[6] Laura de Albizu Campos, *Albizu Campos y la Independencia de Puerto Rico.*

[7] Medina Ramírez, *El Movimiento Libertador en la Historia de Puerto Rico.*

[8] Meyer, *Vito Marcantonio: Radical Politician 1902-1954.*

[9] Rubenstein, ed., *I Vote My Conscience.*

[10] Rosado, *Las Llamas de la Aurora.*

[11] Center for Puerto Rican Studies Library and Archives, *Oral History, The Ruth M. Reynolds Papers.*

[12] Medina Ramírez, *El Movimiento Libertador en la Historia de Puerto Rico.*

[13] For more on the Nationalist Insurrection of 1950, see Chapter 28.

[14] Center for Puerto Rican Studies Library and Archives, *Oral History, The Ruth M. Reynolds Papers.*

[15] Rosado, *Las Llamas de la Aurora.*

Sixth Period — Second Nationalist Party Era

Chapter 26: Defying The Rule Of Empire

Returning To Puerto Rico's Revolution

Unlike in 1930 when he returned to Puerto Rico from his political tour of Latin America, when Don Pedro returned this time, he was welcomed by a gathering of thousands of supporters in one of the largest receptions in Puerto Rico's history. After stepping off the SS Kathryn, he spoke to the crowd of a vow he made while recovering:

> *"That if God allowed me the grace to return to this blessed land, I would wholeheartedly forgive all the insult and slander that could have been done to my person."*

The rest of the day was filled with events attended by Don Pedro, as well as events taking place elsewhere that he did not attend. One event at the University of Puerto Rico, where students raised the Puerto Rican flag at the campus' tower, resulted in three of the students being expelled from the university marking the first act of repression connected to Don Pedro's return to Puerto Rico.

From the port, Don Pedro and his supporters made their way to the Cathedral of San Juan for a religious service organized to give thanks for his safe return to Puerto Rico. From there, they went to the Sixto Escobar Stadium where a rally was held, and many nationalist leaders spoke. Don Pedro told the audience:

> *"I come to say to you that it is the hour of decision. The hour of resolving has come to you, and this hour is non-deferrable. We live through a tragic hour in the life of humanity."*

He also recognized the spirit of Puerto Rico's patriots, saying:

"I don't believe in death. As I do not believe in death, I greet the heroes and martyrs of the homeland present here."

It became very clear that Don Pedro returned to Puerto Rico with every intention of continuing the struggle for national independence. Many things had changed in Puerto Rico, and as the months went on, he spoke to these changes.[1] Don Pedro also made clear that he did not return to give countless speeches, but because his duty was to be in his homeland. On one occasion he explained:

"I came here because I don't believe in voluntary exile... no one should shy away from the sick and crippled mother, because that is when she needs the love of her children most."

The next period of the nationalist movement under Don Pedro's leadership had begun. The very next day after returning, in his first press conference and interview with reporters, Don Pedro stated:

"[The Party] would exhaust all peaceful means in the struggle for independence, and if the United States were to recognize such by those means, that would be most desirable. If, on the other hand, the United States decided to suppress Puerto Ricans' rights by force, then the Nationalist Party would use force to achieve its objectives."

Resisting The Colonial Design

Following World War 2, a reality of widespread poverty and hunger existed throughout Puerto Rico. Colonial authorities began forcing the emigration of Puerto Ricans to the U.S. and developing a series of projects, known collectively as Operation Bootstrap, aimed at transforming Puerto Rico's agrarian economy into an industrial economy. Many living in the countryside and mountains moved into the urban centers, and many living in the urban centers moved to the U.S.

Probably the most dramatic displacement took place on the island of Vieques. In order to maintain U.S. influence in the Atlantic region, entire families on two-thirds of the island of Vieques were violently evicted from their homes to make way for U.S. Navy training grounds and weapons storage facilities. The same day Don Pedro returned to Puerto Rico from his exile he pointed out Vieques, saying, "What has happened in Vieques is what is going to happen throughout the national territory of Puerto Rico." Before the month was over, he visited Vieques and made further statements to the press about the violent displacement there.

On January 12, 1948, an article written by Don Pedro was published in *El Imparcial* under the title "The Destruction of the Island of Vieques by the United States." In it he points out that "Vieques was always a genuinely Puerto Rican community," that, "in possession of all its natural wealth, sustained its population with its own agricultural resources, livestock, food crops and sugar products amounting to more than 20,000 tons per year."[2] Setting up this context for the readers, he then asks the question:

> *"Why has the United States chosen Vieques to repeat in the full light of contemporary civilization the crime of genocide, that is, the deliberate physical or cultural destruction of a nationality?"*

As a general focus after his return, Don Pedro emphasized the need to defy the rule of colonialism in Puerto Rico and work towards establishing Puerto Rico as an independent, sovereign nation with control over its own national matters and interests. During his exile, the *Partido Popular Democrático*—with Luis Muñoz Marín as its president—had begun to gain the support of a large sector of the population.

To do this, their organization began addressing the economic situation of Puerto Rico. They also very explicitly put the question of Puerto Rico's status to the side. As part of this effort, the Popular Democratic Party sought to develop a model that later became the '*Estado Libre Asociado*' design—a status that did not change the colonial situation. This became a key focus of Don Pedro after his return.

Don Pedro, absolutely committed to the nationalist cause, did not waste any time making clear his desire for other political leaders to be as honest and open about their motives as he was with his. During a speech on January 11, 1948, he outlined his thoughts with respect to Muñoz Marín, who had supported independence in the past, saying, "All I ask Luis Muñoz Marín to do is say whether he is Puerto Rican or Yankee; if he is in favor of independence or is against independence."

Repression Of Don Pedro By All Means

From the moment he returned to Puerto Rico, and over the next three years, Don Pedro did not relent in his anti-colonial work. More emphatically and urgently than ever, he spoke about the immediate need for revolution. Seeing the large amount of support Don Pedro had, and the progress he was making towards reorganizing a Nationalist Party that suffered in his absence, U.S. officials began serious efforts to repress him.

Everywhere Don Pedro went he was followed, and when his wife and family joined him in April 1948 the same became true for them. First at the Normandy Hotel, and then outside their home in Old San Juan, agents rotated in shifts to keep him under constant, round-the-clock surveillance. They did this without being discreet at all. Even the people that visited Don Pedro, or that he visited, were approached and interrogated soon afterwards by agents.[3]

Don Pedro was openly defiant of the surveillance of him and other nationalists, which many felt was aimed at provoking them. In a speech delivered in Ponce on March 21, 1949, he warned U.S. officials, saying:

> *"I warn these gentlemen that this thing about investigating where the most humble of nationalists eats, sleeps, and works is something that has to end... We're human, we're very patient, but one day we're going to run out of patience, we're going to run out of patience one day and the situation is going to be a little delicate and there's going to be a lot of gunshots here. Yes, they're talking about the violence of the nationalists. Who are the violent ones here? The United States government."*

By the time he made this statement a law had been passed—which he knew about and which he also defied—that was later used to arrest thousands of Puerto Ricans. Law 53,[4] put in effect on June 10, 1948, and known as 'the Gag Law,' was understood to be a tool to target Don Pedro, the Nationalist Party, and any pro-independence sentiment or dissent in Puerto Rico. As a result of the work of agents to record/transcribe every speech he gave, when Don Pedro was arrested again in 1950 the violations brought against him under the Gag Law were a series of twelve speeches he delivered.[5]

Before his arrest in 1950, however, signs pointed to a much more serious threat faced by Don Pedro in the form of a possible assassination attempt. As Muñoz Marín worked with U.S. officials to draft a law to establish a commonwealth government in Puerto Rico, word made way to Don Pedro of a plan to either use the military to arrest nationalist leaders en masse or to assassinate them if such arrests could not be achieved. This plan, according to Ruth Reynolds, was shared with Muñoz Marín by the U.S. secretary of defense who identified the plan as a measure to ensure the commonwealth law[6] would not be opposed.

On September 23, 1950, Don Pedro again disregarded the Gag Law and all the intimidation and threats he was facing. In an event commemorating *El Grito de Lares* he delivered a speech in the 'altar of the homeland' and reacted to the colonial formula that U.S. and collaborating officials were seeking to impose upon Puerto Rico. His words were clear and simple: "All this must be challenged only as the men of Lares challenged despotism, with revolution."

In May 1950, Don Pedro entrusted his wife, with the support of devoted nationalist Juan Juarbe Juarbe, to travel to Cuba and take on the task of notifying the leaders and organizations of the Latin American countries of the plans to assassinate him. At the same time, during this campaign they were to also make every effort to secure arms and other materials for use in the revolt now being planned in Puerto Rico.[7]

Chapter 27: Speaking Truth To Power[8]

Dr. Manuel de la Pila Iglesias

Many are the stories of Pedro Albizu Campos that portray the impact of his character. While going through the oral history with Ruth Reynolds held at the Center for Puerto Rican Studies (Hunter College, CUNY), I came across one that particularly grabbed my attention.[9] Related to Ruth by Don Pedro in later years, it took place in early October 1950 in Ponce. The occasion was the passing of 65-year-old Dr. Manuel de la Pila Iglesias, a significant medical figure in Puerto Rico who grew up and based his practice in Ponce.

Born November 16, 1882, in Spain, Dr. Manuel de la Pila Iglesias was brought by his mother to Ponce three years later after the death of his father and brother. Attending university for medicine in both Ponce and Barcelona, Dr. Pila went on to study in several other countries and cities. The clinic in Ponce he established in 1925 became the *Hospital Metropolitano Dr. Pila* that still runs today. Going on to found organizations and influence the passing of Puerto Rico's first health insurance legislature, Dr. Pila was recognized by the Catholic Church and knighted into the Order of Saint Gregory by Pope Pio XI on November 15, 1930. Chosen to be part of a group tasked to develop a study on the possibility of opening a medical school in the University of Puerto Rico, his work helped pave the way for the medical schools now existing today in Puerto Rico. Known as *el Médico de Médicos*, he died suddenly on October 5, 1950 in an automobile accident.[10]

Speaking Truth To Power

Due to the high standing of Dr. Pila in Ponce, most of the local economic and political elite showed up to his funeral services to pay respects to the life of their distinguished peer. Among this group of notables was Don Pedro. As Don Pedro casually mingled with all of them, someone finally asked him, "What do you feel about the future economically of this country?" Don Pedro calculated his words and said:

> *"We can judge the future in terms of the past. You and you and you and I were boys together. We didn't all know each other... but we went through the same period here in Ponce. And we got to know each other a little bit later. My father was a property owner. So was yours, so was yours, so was yours."*

Don Pedro continued in this way, inquiring into the current status of each family. All had lost the land they once owned. One ran a candy factory under constant threat of price wars. All had sent their sons to the United States for their education. Two of their sons stayed to work in managerial positions, while the other worked in a managerial position for an American company in Ponce.

Don Pedro left his small audience in a silence when he concluded:

> *"Your fathers were property owners, you professional businessmen, but in charge of your own lives. Your sons, no. So what is that future of this country economically, if it does not have independence?*
>
> *There comes a time in the history of every country when the propertied classes, those who have felt it to their convenience to cooperate with the regime, they come to realize that if not for their own sakes, for the sake of their children and their grandchildren, they have to take a different stand. Are you gentlemen approaching that time?"*

Honoring The Fallen

Privately a supporter of the independence of Puerto Rico, Dr. Pila wished that in death his position on the status question be recognized. For this reason, his widow directly asked Don Pedro to provide the funeral oration on the following day, which he agreed to do.

With the political and economic elite again in attendance, several gave speeches. A priest urged the audience to pray that Dr. Pila should not spend much time in purgatory. Another person spoke of all the virtues of a doctor that Dr. Pila exemplified.

Then, Don Pedro began speaking, quickly grabbing everyone's attention:

> *"We've heard some remarks on the virtues of Dr. Pila, but everyone knows I would not be here if he had not made contributions in another sphere... Now he was a Spaniard by birth, he was not a Puerto Rican by birth, but his contribution... to Puerto Rico's freedom has been greater than that of almost anyone in Ponce. And that must be recognized in death.*
>
> *We've heard priests, we've been urged to pray for the soul of Dr. Pila that he may not remain long in purgatory. I tell you today that today Dr. Pila is sitting at the right hand of God and we should pray to Dr. Pila for ourselves that he may intervene for us so that we may not have to spend [a] long time in purgatory."*

Stunned, one of the previous speakers fainted and had to be carried away.

Such was the impact of the presence and words of Pedro Albizu Campos. He spoke truth to power with a clarity able to penetrate the core of all bearing witness. In the story above, he spoke convincingly of the need to make personal sacrifices to end the economic domination of Puerto Rico by the United States, and as a first step in asserting the nation's right to independence. He also spoke of the honor in dying as a supporter of Puerto Rico's independence, even if one's support of such in life was not particularly visible.

What is interesting about this event is that it is taking place in a moment when both surveillance on Don Pedro and tension between the government and the Nationalist Party is at its height. Just a few weeks later, Don Pedro would order the start of an island-wide revolt that also resulted in an armed attack on the president of the United States.

Chapter 28: The Nationalist Insurrection Of 1950

Sparking The Fire Of Revolt

By the time Don Pedro spoke on September 23, 1950 in Lares, nationalists were aware of an intent to assassinate him and arrest other leaders en masse. Colonial officials, thanks to informants, knew the Nationalist Party was preparing to stage an armed revolt. On June 11, Party members were on high alert during a political event, believing firmly that a plot to arrest Don Pedro was going to be carried out—this arrest did not take place. In the early morning hours of October 27, the actions of colonial officials were serious enough to cause the nationalist movement to become activated in exactly the way colonial officials hoped to prevent.

After a radio-broadcasted celebration in Fajardo of the birthday of Puerto Rico-born Antonio Valero de Bernabé—a general in Simón Bolívar's army—nationalists escorting Don Pedro back to San Juan were followed by three cars of undercover agents. When the agents began trying to force Don Pedro's car to the side of the road, the other two cars made maneuvers that allowed his car to get away. The two cars were eventually stopped at separate locations in Santurce at 3:15AM and 3:30AM. The search of one of the cars resulted in the seizure of two .37-caliber guns, five Molotov cocktails, and a Thompson submachine gun, with an additional number of Molotov cocktails seized in the second vehicle.[11]

When Don Pedro heard about the arrests a few hours later he knew it was only a matter of time before police came to arrest or kill him. Facing such alternatives, and clear that U.S. officials would conspire by any means, as they had in the past, to ensure he was convicted in court and sentenced to many years, Don Pedro decided to order the start of what became the Nationalist Insurrection of 1950. His order to initiate the uprising at noon on October 30 was dispersed across the nationalist network. Over the next few days armed confrontations took place throughout Puerto Rico, with an additional armed action taking place in Washington, D.C.

The morning of October 28, a prison break in which 110 people escaped from the '*Oso Blanco*' penitentiary in Río Piedras created a further concern for officials. Initiated by an incarcerated person with no apparent nationalist ties, the riot that followed and led to the actual escape was in part led by a nationalist in the prison that had received visits from high-ranking Nationalist Party members in the days prior. This prison break, forcing police to focus on capturing the people who escaped, postponed plans to arrest Party members and raid their homes. [12]

Once focus returned to the nationalists, police were overwhelmed, and the National Guard was called in to support them. One of the first actions taken by the National Guard was to occupy and close major roads.

The Courage And Sacrifice Of Los Decididos [13]

With the U.S. government having the most powerful military in the world, the struggle of the nationalists was not about having a military conflict but about taking a moral stand against the idea and system of colonial-imperialism. From the start of Don Pedro's leadership within the Nationalist Party he always stressed the undeniable place of courage and sacrifice within the revolutionary struggle, and the need for members to be willing to sacrifice life and property if necessary. After the first encounter between nationalists and police in Peñuelas at 3AM on October 30, many nationalists—as well as communists and supporters of the *Partido Independentista Puertorriqueño* [14]—decided to accept the many risks involved and join the uprising.

Peñuelas and Ponce

In Peñuelas, a small group of nationalists engaged in a shootout with about 31 police officers arriving to raid a farm identified by informants as a location of arms. Three nationalists were killed. In neighboring Ponce, at 10AM, a nationalist that escaped the shootout in Peñuelas led another group in transporting arms to Utuado. They were intercepted and engaged in a shootout that left a police colonel dead.

Arecibo

In Arecibo, at 11AM, one group of seven nationalists attacked a police station and killed four officers. One of the nationalists died while covering the escape of the others who were later arrested by the National Guard. Another group in Arecibo composed of 15 nationalists decided to head to Utuado but were dispersed when it was clear the National Guard controlled the major roads. A third group that stayed in Arecibo had a shootout with National Guard soldiers in Muñoz Rivera Park that resulted in the death of one nationalist. A fourth group used a vehicle to drive by and shoot at buildings occupied by the National Guard.

Utuado

In Utuado, around noon, a group of 32 nationalists split up and attacked the federal post office and local police station. As the first group approached their target, they were shot at in front of a Catholic Church by police stationed in the nearby plaza. A few nationalists managed to run ahead and successfully set the post office on fire. After firefighters arrived at the post office, an argument that developed resulted in another shootout in which one of the firemen was shot and killed.

The group attacking the police station encountered a police force waiting in prepared battle positions. About a dozen nationalists fled to the nearby house of a Party member and took up a position there, returning fire as police unleashed a hail of bullets on the residence for two hours.

After sunset, around 8PM, over 1,000 National Guard soldiers arrived on the scene. They set up positions with machine guns and fired on the house at 11PM and again at 1130PM. Overwhelmed by the force, with one nationalist already dead, the remaining nationalists surrendered and were marched by the National Guard towards the police station. At 1AM, on October 31, the troops stopped short of the police station, forced their prisoners into an alley, and proceeded to shoot them with machine-guns as people watched from their windows.

Four died immediately and five others were left for dead, with doctors not arriving until hours later. The event became known as the Utuado Massacre. Later that same day, after the National Guard troops left Utuado, four National Guard planes began targeted bombings of buildings and farms in the town.

San Juan

In San Juan, the local commander of the Liberation Army, Raimundo Díaz Pacheco, led an attack at noon on October 30 with four other nationalists on the Governor's Mansion, '*La Fortaleza*', hoping to take the governor hostage. Met with an expecting and prepared police force, all except one of the nationalists, Gregorio Hernández, were killed within an hour of the vehicle stopping in the main entrance area. At the same time, a group of nationalists joined with university students and attacked the police station and federal courthouse in two separate actions, both producing a shootout that resulted in only a few injuries. Yet another attack, on the federal courthouse in Santurce's Barrio Obrero, resulted in two National Guard troops being injured.

The following day, on October 31, a sensational event occurred at *Salón Boricua*, the barbershop of Don Pedro's personal barber Vidal Santiago Díaz. Around 2PM, confronted by a policeman, his decision to defend himself resulted in a shootout with, what would eventually be, fifteen policemen backed by 25 National Guard troops armed with machine-guns, rifles, revolvers, and grenades.

In a brief period before the shootout when police and troops were still gathering outside, Santiago Díaz placed weapons throughout the barber shop. Tactically returning fire from several windows and both floors of the structure, he gave the impression that there were more combatants inside than just himself. During the gunfight, which lasted three hours, several mobile radio units arrived and began transmitting the event live across Puerto Rico. When asked by a reporter how many people were inside *Salón Boricua*, a lieutenant estimated 20-30. When the gunfight finally ended after a final coordinated police/National Guard attack, several bystanders were counted among the injured and, even after being shot in the head at point blank range and receiving several wounds, Santiago Díaz survived and became a minor celebrity.

Mayagüez

In Mayagüez, the large group of over 40 nationalists prepared to fight were divided into five smaller groups, each with five separate missions. Due to technical issues with their explosives, and the fact that they did not move into action until 2PM on October 30, by which time authorities had already situated themselves into defensive positions, none of their activities resulted in any success.

A second attack on the local police station in the evening resulted in a few injuries on both sides, in addition to three civilians. One of the groups, which planned to attack police in the morning of October 31, were instead attacked by police as they were preparing to move out. This group returned fire and escaped to the nearby mountains.

Washington, D.C.

In New York City, on October 29, a relative of several participants of the uprising in Jayuya, Griselio Torresola, brought a newspaper article to the home of the president of the New York chapter of the Nationalist Party, Oscar Collazo. Showing him the article, they both discussed the events taking place in Puerto Rico. Knowing this was the beginning of the insurrection that was being planned, they both took a train to Washington, D.C. to stage an attack on U.S. President Harry Truman.

Arriving in D.C. on October 30, they used the rest of that day and the next to plan their mission, which they accepted would probably result in their death. Taking a taxi to the Blair House, the temporary residence of the president, at 2:20PM on November 1 they began their attack.

Collazo, who had been quickly trained by Griselio on how to use his weapon, was quickly out of the fight when his weapon jammed. Griselio was able to mortally wound a guard stationed in a booth but was then killed when the same guard returned a fatal shot. Within a few minutes, Griselio was killed, and Collazo was shot in the chest and rendered unconscious.

Naranjito

In Naranjito, nationalists were led by a World War 2 veteran, José Antonio Negrón, in an attack on the local police station at 12noon on October 30.

Expected by police and met with gunfire, the group of seven nationalists retreated into the mountains. From there they led an unexpected guerrilla campaign in which they hid and defended their position by day and conducted attacks by night. The reputation of Negrón as being a person always willing to help those in need, and who did not drink or gamble, allowed him to receive the support of locals without being snitched on as his group moved discreetly throughout Naranjito. This continued until November 6 when Negrón was separated from the rest of his group when they were arrested by National Guard troops. Negrón, by himself, continued resisting and evading capture until November 10, officially putting an end to the insurrection.

Jayuya And The Second Declaration Of Independence

The events that took place in Jayuya stand out among everything else that took place in the insurrection. This is so clear that some who have written about the Nationalist Insurrection of 1950 instead labeled it '*El Grito de Jayuya*' or the 'Jayuya Uprising.' In some of these writings only the events that specifically took place in Jayuya are covered, but in some writings the events in Jayuya are centered while only giving a mention to 'other events' that took place elsewhere in Puerto Rico. In any case, the key success of the nationalist movement in Jayuya was the declaration, for the second time in history since 1868 Lares, of Puerto Rico as a free, independent republic.

Hearing news over the radio about what was happening in Arecibo as they were preparing their weapons, the nationalists in Jayuya proceeded with their plans at noon on October 30. One group, led by another World War 2 veteran named Carlos Irizarry, made their way to the local police station and engaged in a shootout that both mortally wounded Irizarry and forced the police to flee—one policeman was also killed.

Taking over leadership of the group from that point forward was Elio Torresola, the brother of Griselio Torresola. Elio and his group went on to burn down the police station and then headed to the post office, which they also burned down. At their last target, the records of the selective service related to military recruitment, they removed all records and materials from the selective service building and lit them on fire in the street, careful to prevent the burning of an adjacent theater.

While this was going on, nationalist leader Blanca Canales led another group to the town's telephone station. They confronted the telephone operator and were able to cut the telephone lines without incident, preventing news of what was happening in Jayuya from spreading to colonial officials.

After completing this mission, Canales and her group headed to the town plaza where she raised the flag of Puerto Rico on the balcony of a hotel and declared Puerto Rico a free republic. After a crowd began to form, she gave a small speech explaining the purpose of the revolution and the desire of the nationalists to unite the country against colonial rule.

The following day, on October 31, the National Guard began an air-bombing campaign targeting Jayuya's infrastructure, mountains, and sugar plantations, going on from there to do the same in Utuado, as previously mentioned. Able to maintain control of Jayuya for three days, the nationalists surrendered on November 2 when National Guard reinforcements began to arrive.[15]

What happened in Jayuya during the Nationalist Insurrection of 1950 is of great symbolic and historical importance. The armed revolt was part of a much larger effort, led ideologically by Don Pedro, to resist colonialism in Puerto Rico. Recent developments coauthored by Luis Muñoz Marín and endorsed by President Truman were going to result in a strengthening of the factors that hold the structure of colonialism in place. The insurrection was the nationalist response to this.[16]

Chapter 29: Focus And Preparation Of The Revolt

Changes In The Colonial Design

The main point of contention for Don Pedro during the period of 1947-1950 was the series of political efforts that led to Public Law 600.[17] This law, signed and enacted by President Truman on July 3, 1950, allowed for a June 1951 referendum where Puerto Ricans would vote for or against the drafting of their own constitution and the forming of a new government. The development of this law began as early as 1945 when Puerto Rico's legislature created the Legislative Commission on the Political Status of Puerto Rico, presided over by Luis Muñoz Marín.

In 1946, this Status Commission began proposing a third status option besides statehood and independence. It was called the *Pueblo Asociado de Puerto Rico*. The following year, U.S. Congress approved, and President Truman signed a measure that allowed Puerto Ricans, for the first time, to elect their own governor.[18] With Muñoz Marín winning the election in 1948 and assuming office as the first elected governor on January 2, 1949, he very quickly began working on the new colonial formula.

This new formula was finalized in March 1950 as the *Estado Libre Asociado*, or Commonwealth of Puerto Rico in English. It would go in effect if it received a majority of votes in the 1951 referendum.

Don Pedro heard about all these developments while in exile, and then firsthand after his return to Puerto Rico. He said the referendum, "like everything that the United States government sponsors in Puerto Rico–is just a trap for Puerto Ricans to keep spinning the wheel."[19] Getting to the heart of the issue, Don Pedro said the following about the proposed constitution:

"What they seek with that constitution is to validate the current relations—a relationship of force that began on July 25, 1898 with the invasion of the Puerto Rican national territory—to present themselves before the world pretending to have clean hands. They speak of a covenant, a covenant with a people kept in slavery!"

Revolutionary Organization And Planning

The Nationalist Party was organized generally the same as it had been in the past, with Don Pedro at the head of both its military and civil components. During the uprising, the Party's military had Tomás López de Victoria as its commander, with sub-commanders in San Juan, Humacao, Cayey, Ponce, Mayagüez, Utuado, and Arecibo.

Local chapters also had captains—Don Pedro's barber Vidal Santiago Díaz, for example, was a captain in San Juan. The New York chapter of the Party was known to be successful in acquiring funds used to buy weapons and other materials.[20]

Several farms throughout Puerto Rico were used as training grounds for nationalist militants to learn target shooting, gain experience with the effects of explosive and incendiary bombs, and conduct battle drills. Some of these battle drills—such as squad attack, react to contact, break contact, react to near and far ambush—were taken directly from U.S. Army field manuals obtained from discreet associates within the 65th Infantry Regiment, known as the Borinqueneers.[21]

The events that would take place from the end of October to the beginning of November 1950 was the nationalist response to everything transpiring.[22] Originally set to take place at a later date, the uprising was ordered for noon on October 30 by Don Pedro because the mass arrest and possible assassination of nationalist leaders was felt to be imminent. After a series of arrests, raids, and shootouts in Peñuelas and Ponce, it was decided that the developing situation had to be protested and a statement had to be made before such arrests or killings could take place.

With nationalists losing the element of surprise, police learning from informants the location of weapon stashes, and the uprising being ordered suddenly and ahead of schedule, the nationalist resistance faced great challenges. Despite this, nationalists still attempted to follow the plans that had been developed as best as they could.

First, they were to attack police stations and locations of National Guard troops in their respective towns and burn federal post office buildings and all records held in selective service offices. After these actions took place, nationalist forces were to make their way to Utuado where, with the support of the town's well-developed agricultural and livestock supply, they could continue their resistance for as long as a month.

The United Nations

The reason Don Pedro planned for nationalist resistance to be centered in Utuado, making use of that town's ability to support a drawn-out struggle, is because he hoped the resistance could hold on long enough to influence the General Assembly of the United Nations to become involved and intervene in favor of the independence of Puerto Rico.[23] Knowing a defeat of the U.S. military was not feasible, Don Pedro hoped to use international pressure to force the U.S. government to cease any military response to the uprising, recognize Puerto Rico as an independent nation, and begin the process of decolonization.

Thelma Mielke, a North American anti-imperialist activist from New York, had been active in the UN on behalf of Puerto Rico's independence since it was founded in 1945 and the Nationalist Party was given status as a non-governmental organization. Serving as the Party's UN delegate, Mielke worked tirelessly to raise international awareness around Puerto Rico, providing delegates regular information on its colonial status.

On October 31, after news of the events began to be publicized, Mielke wrote the UN secretary general informing him of the events and requesting that Puerto Rico's case be presented before the UN Security Council.

Failing to receive a response, on November 2 Mielke went to the UN with a copy of the letter. The response given by a UN spokesperson was that the events were a "local affair," and that "in the United States' view the case could not be brought before the world organization."[24] On November 6, she received a letter from the head of the UN Committee on Non-Governmental Organizations that very simply said her observer status in the UN was canceled. It read: "Your pass is no longer valid."

Don Pedro knew Chapter 11 of the UN Charter mandated all members "which have or assume responsibilities for the administration of territories whose peoples have not yet attained a full measure of self-government recognize the principle that the interests of the inhabitants of these territories are paramount." He also knew that the influence of the colonial powers within the UN was significant.

In an interview published on January 4, 1948, he called the U.S. and these colonial powers "a united front for a restricted interpretation of Chapter 11." He also highlighted three reports the U.S. submitted to the UN on the conditions in Puerto Rico. These reports were submitted to fulfill the obligation under Article 73 of Chapter 11, which requires colonial powers to provide regular, detailed reports on any non-self-governing territories under their responsibility.[25]

Allowing Puerto Ricans to elect their own governor and vote for the establishment of a constitutional government was part of the U.S. political strategy to portray Puerto Rico as having achieved self-government as mandated by the UN Charter. Clearly, as implied in the response given to Mielke when she visited the UN, in the aftermath of the nationalist uprising in Puerto Rico, the U.S. government quickly moved to influence the narrative held by UN representatives in their favor. While the case of colonialism in Puerto Rico would continue to be raised there, these events ended the official representation of the Nationalist Party as a non-governmental organization within the UN and, not long after, the responsibility of the U.S. to report yearly on the status of Puerto Rico.

Chapter 30: The Arrest Of A Nation

The Siege Of Don Pedro's Residence

After Don Pedro evaded police in the early morning of October 27 he made his way to the headquarters of the Nationalist Party located at 156 *Calle Sol* between *Calle Cruz* and *Calle San José* in Old San Juan—the building also served as his residence. He stayed there, quietly awaiting the commencement of his orders. When October 30 arrived, inside with him were two nationalists, Doris Torresola and Carmen María Pérez, and outside was a growing force of dozens of heavily armed officers and soldiers with snipers on rooftops. The nationalists stacked books in front of the windows and returned fire when police began their assault.

During the initial exchange of gunfire, Doris Torresola was shot in the neck. Right after the exchange ended, a 20-year-old university student and nationalist, Juan José Muñoz Matos, thinking everyone inside had been killed, avoided police and made his way into the residence where he was immediately given a weapon. Since the bleeding of Torresola's wound was not going to be easily stopped with the towels on hand, a half hour after Muñoz Matos arrived Don Pedro ordered him and Carmen María to carry her outside. Left alone, during the moment when the three nationalists were exiting the building and being placed under arrest, Don Pedro heard the familiar voice of another nationalist, Alvaro Rivera Walker, who took advantage of the tense situation and entered the building to join him.

Rivera Walker and Don Pedro spent the night keeping watch of the windows and stairs of the building, resting as they could between sporadic gunfire. They had only a small supply of water and canned sardines that Don Pedro happened to have.

The next morning of October 31, when the chief of police began communicating with them on a bullhorn, they cautiously made their way to the outside balcony. Don Pedro confronted the forces gathered and directly asked who had been shooting at his residence overnight. He also asked about the status of Doris Torresola and about the shooting of Efraín López. Efraín had escaped from prison and was shot while trying to enter Don Pedro's residence, apparently to deliver him a message, eventually dying as a result of his gunshot wounds. Receiving no answers to his questions, Rivera Walker and Don Pedro returned inside.

In the early morning of November 2, shortly after midnight, police and National Guard forces finally made their move to arrest Don Pedro. It was understood that Don Pedro had been kept alive up to that point as part of an order to avoid turning him into a martyr of the movement. After a barrage of shots from machine-guns and other weapons, several tear-gas grenades were shot into the residence. Choked and blinded by the gas, Alvaro Walker and Don Pedro eventually surrendered and were carried, semi-conscious, into police custody at 3:15AM.

When Don Pedro was visited later that day in police headquarters by reporters hoping to take pictures and hear from him, he appeared weak and disheveled. His eyes were still swollen from the tear-gas, and his eyelids greasy from the menthol ointment he used to alleviate its effects. Dressed in slippers, dark pants, and a blue long-sleeved nightshirt with stripes, he greeted reporters with a smile, thanked them for coming, and offered only the following words: "I will say that the Homeland is going through its glorious transfiguration."[26]

Mass Political Incarceration And Abuse

After the shooting in Washington, D.C., Governor Muñoz Marín declared martial law—without issuing a public declaration. Throughout Puerto Rico the police and National Guard not only arrested those who actively participated in the uprising, but they also began to seek out and arrest countless others who had not. The reason given for most of these arrests was the supposed investigation into the participants of the revolt. Among those arrested were nationalists, non-nationalist independence supporters, and even people that were not independence supporters by any means.[27]

Dozens of people, including children, were lined up and marched through the streets at gunpoint to jail. Some who had been taken out of bed arrived in pajamas. There was no legal process in just about every case, no bail set, and it is even known that some people were arrested because of personal grudges that police informants had against them. According to police data, 1,006 people were "preventively arrested."

Held for almost a week, about 800 were released on November 6, all said to have been detained as witnesses. Not surprisingly, their release came just one day after the registration of new voters had taken place, an event that Muñoz Marín wanted to ensure would not be affected by any acts of opposition.

Conditions faced by those arrested were clear cases of abuse motivated by the political nature of their cause. Author Nelson A. Denis details some of these conditions: "Bright light bulbs shined in their cells twenty-four hours a day. They were given no sheets, towels, or toilet paper; no showers were allowed for three weeks; visitors and correspondence were prohibited. The leaders were all placed in solitary confinement... Their meals were often half-cooked rice, old bread, and wormy pig's feet... Their experiences—strip searches, cavity searches, sleep deprivation, starvation, isolation, and humiliation—were engineered to destroy their dignity and break their spirits."[28]

In New York City, the wife of Oscar Collazo, Rosa Cortez, and the widow of Griselio Torresola, Carmen Otero, were both arrested. Thirteen others, including Collazo's three daughters, were questioned and issued subpoenas to appear before a Federal Grand Jury.[29]

Sentences faced by nationalists ranged widely. Rosa Cortez and Carmen Otero, despite not actually being charged with anything, were both incarcerated for two months; Blanca Canales was sentenced to life imprisonment; and Oscar Collazo was given a death sentence later commuted to life imprisonment.[30] The trials were unfair and resulted in clearly political judgments.[31]

The most eventful trial was that of 20-year-old nationalist Olga Viscal Garriga who refused to accept the authority of the courts in Puerto Rico to judge her political actions. She repeatedly interrupted the prosecutor and judge, at one point saying, "It's not too late to go back to La Fortaleza!" Viscal Garriga received 31 charges of contempt of court, was convicted for violating the Gag Law, and was finally sentenced to one to ten years in prison plus 31 months for her contempt of court charges.[32]

Constitutional Colonialism

The Gag Law was created specifically as a tool to silence and imprison nationalists and other independence supporters. Muñoz Marín was forewarned just before the passing of Public Law 600 of plans to arrest, if not assassinate, nationalist opposition to that law. All of this makes clear that the U.S. government made every effort to complete the masking of its colonial control over Puerto Rico. It is within this context—with Don Pedro and countless other nationalist leaders imprisoned, and many other leaders having been killed—that Public Law 600 unfolded to its conclusion.[33]

First, in June 1951 when there was a total of 776,000 registered voters, the law was passed with 387,016 people (49.9% of registered voters) voting in its favor, with 119,169 voting against, and 269,815 abstaining. Then, in March 1952 when there was a total of 783,610 registered voters, the proposed constitution received a passing vote with 373,594 (47.1% of registered voters) favorable votes, with 82,877 voting against, and 327,139 abstaining. On July 25, 1952, the constitution went into effect, establishing the Commonwealth of Puerto Rico or 'Free Associated State.' Changing nothing of Puerto Rico's colonial reality, the constitution left intact key sections of the 1917 Jones Act that gave the U.S. Congress plenary power over Puerto Rico.

The colony had been effectively masked before the international community, the U.S. government no longer had to send yearly reports to the UN, and Puerto Rico was argued to have arrived at self-government. During this entire period, and until the U.S. Supreme Court ruled it unconstitutional in 1957, the Gag Law remained in effect.

In this atmosphere of severe political repression and abuse, the colonial formula largely spearheaded by Muñoz Marín had no real opposition. The foremost opposition leader, Don Pedro, charged with violating the Gag Law, was convicted on August 15, 1951 and sentenced on August 29, 1951 to serve at least 12 and no more than 54 years.[34] Many nationalists remained in prison until 1972 when they were pardoned by the governor of Puerto Rico at the time. Oscar Collazo was released in 1979 when U.S. President Jimmy Carter commuted his sentence.

Charge	Violation	Date & Location	Sentence
One	Public speech	25 Jul. 1948, Guánica	1-2 years
Two	Public speech	21 Mar. 1949, Ponce	1-3 years
Three	Public speech	8 Apr. 1949, Cabo Rojo	1-4 years
Four	Public speech	25 Jul. 1949, Guánica	1-5 years
Five	Public speech	23 Sep. 1949, Lares	1-5 years
Six	Public speech	18 Dec. 1949, Arecibo	1-5 years
Seven	Public speech	23 Feb. 1950, Utuado	1-5 years
Eight	Public speech	21 Mar. 1950, Ponce	1-5 years
Nine	Public speech	18 Apr. 1950, Cabo Rojo	1-5 years
Ten	Public speech	16 Apr. 1950, Santurce	1-5 years
Eleven	Public speech	11 Jun. 1950, Manatí	1-5 years
Twelve	Public speech	23 Sep. 1950, Lares	1-5 years

Don Pedro's Felony Violations Under The Gag Law

Chapter 31: A Law And Era To Be Remembered

The Gag Law

Passed on May 21, 1948, and enacted on June 10, 1948, the Gag Law made it a felony to maintain a belief in or work towards the "overthrowing, paralyzing or destroying [of] the Insular Government or any of its subdivisions by means of force or violence."[35] One of the many criticisms of the law was the fact that it was essentially an English translation, almost word for word, of parts of the Alien Registration Act of 1940, also known as the Smith Act. Because this federal law was assumed to also cover Puerto Rico, many questioned why it needed to also be codified—duplicated—within the colonial government.

From the perspective of the U.S. government, the law was a source of relief as it was very clear that, not wishing to repeat 1936, U.S. officials wanted to transfer to the Puerto Rican government the work and responsibility of handling all cases of dissent in Puerto Rico. This would also, they hoped, prevent criticism of the government regarding their role in Puerto Rico and improve their international image. Any cases of dissent in Puerto Rico would be seen as internal matters to be managed by Puerto Rican courts.

Interestingly, one of the Puerto Rican legislators promoting the law said it would also help with "imposing criminal sanctions against those who advise or incite others to commit a felony, even though the felony may not have been committed." Apparently, at the time in Puerto Rico it was "extremely difficult to get a conviction for conspiracy."

Of course, there were other reasons for the development and eventual passing of the Gag Law. In her book on the 1948 law, author Ivonne Acosta essentially points to three main reasons for it being passed: 1) to prevent opposition to the election of the first Puerto Rican governor and counter the growing support for the recently founded Puerto Rican Independence Party; 2) to make possible the establishment of the Commonwealth government by what would appear to be a democratic voting process; 3) to counter the critical attacks in the UN made by the Soviet Union within the context of the emerging Cold War by arguing that Puerto Rico, having elected its own governor and voted for the Commonwealth status, had attained self-government.

Climate Under The Gag Law

Before the Gag Law was enacted on June 10, there was significant protest against it. All four of Puerto Rico's daily newspapers[36] published content in opposition to the law. One of them, *El Universal*, seen as the pro-government publication of Muñoz Marín and his associates, published an editorial on May 22 saying that the law had the potential to become "a terrible weapon against the citizen's rights and the freedom of press and speech." A week later, the newspaper suddenly ceased all operations and, a few months after that, Muñoz Marín started a new publication named *El Diario de Puerto Rico*.

The conservative, pro-American newspaper *El Día* itself said the law "is loaded with dynamite against the civil liberties of the American citizens in Puerto Rico."

On May 25, a large meeting was held in the *Ateneo Puertorriqueño* with multiple representatives attending on behalf of forty-three different entities. The newspaper *El Día* described the participants as "the political, economic, social, labor, civic, religious and professional institutions that unreservedly pledged their support to the protest initiated by the independent press in the country."

After an attempt to disrupt the meeting by supporters of the ruling Popular Democratic Party, everyone present approved a resolution requesting that the governor of Puerto Rico not sign the bill into law. An objection shared at the meeting revolved around the law being approved before an election where Puerto Ricans would elect their own governor for the first time. The objection stressed that those entitled to vote "have the right to cast their ballots freely and in absolute spiritual tranquility."

As previously mentioned, the day after the registration of voters took place on November 5, 1950, some 800 people were released from their imprisonment following the nationalist insurrection. The approximately 200 who remained in prison faced charges under the Gag Law, most of them people identified as Nationalist Party members or sympathizers. Don Pedro was convicted of violating the Gag Law because of a series of speeches. Others were convicted for simply attending nationalist rallies or raising funds for nationalist events.[37]

The Gag Law produced a climate of deep fear in which people weren't sure what could be considered a violation, so they assumed anything could possibly result in their arrest. In May 1951 an organization created in Puerto Rico called the Committee for Civil Liberties published a report that spoke to the terrible economic situation of the families of those in prison, and the difficulty in securing aid for them. It stated: "The rumor has been circulated that activities to collect funds, or even the giving of donations, are violations of the Gag Laws."

Following the 1954 attack on Congress, more arrests for the supposed violation of the Gag Law took place. Reasons for the eventual convictions included being a nationalist, paying rent for offices maintained by the Party, selling tickets for a benefit dance, and attending a Catholic mass in honor of those who died in the 1950 attack on *La Fortaleza*.

A Repealed Law Affecting The Present

In April 1956 a court case in the U.S. involving a communist leader named Steve Nelson influenced a series of events to take place in Puerto Rico that eventually resulted in the Gag Law being repealed. Nelson's 1952 conviction for violating Pennsylvania's state sedition laws was overturned by the Supreme Court, which ruled that the state's sedition law was superseded by the federal Smith Act. Puerto Rican defense lawyers argued in court that if the federal law trumped the local law of the states, then it stands to reason that it also trumps insular Puerto Rican law. On August 1, 1957, the Gag Law was finally repealed.

Shortly before the law was repealed, the newspaper *El Mundo* commented that "it was a true misfortune that in all this time the local discontent had been ignored and that it had waited for the U.S. Supreme Court to de-claw the Smith Act, of which the Gag Law is a poisonous imitation."

It is an important fact worth repeating that the vote for Puerto Rico's first elected governor, and the vote in favor of establishing the Commonwealth status and government that exists today, both took place while the Gag Law was in effect. This establishment of the new and improved colonial status was crucial for industrialization plans that relied on the investment of foreign capital, primarily from the U.S. The reason it was seen as so crucial is because it was felt the new status, backed by the U.S. government, would provide the sense of political stability needed to attract the financial investment to put the plans in motion. Before the Commonwealth government, potential investors were hesitant because of the perceived instability in the territory.

By the time it was repealed, use of the Gag Law as a tool to guarantee the strengthening of the colonial grip had taken place as planned. Not coincidentally, the process of repealing the law occurred right after the November 1956 general elections that saw the victory of Muñoz Marín and the Popular Democratic Party. The results of that election were used by Muñoz Marín to argue the popular acceptance of and stability offered by the newly established Commonwealth government, and to bring attention to the key role he and his political party played.

Author Ivonne Acosta called the Gag Law "one of the most shameful and sad pages of our recent history" that has been "buried in the collective amnesia of our people."[38] Although it is a law and era that has been left out of the popular historical narrative of Puerto Rico, the Gag Law and the climate under it had a significant effect on the generations that followed. The fear it produced around the support of independence created a stigma that continues to influence the way in which the independence movement is viewed today. As an obvious consequence, the law's legacy has also influenced the way in which Don Pedro and other independence leaders are remembered. This effect must be consciously undone.

Chapter 32: Radiation Torture In La Princesa

Political Abuse In The Atomic Age

When Don Pedro was in Atlanta Penitentiary from 1937-1943, the health issues resulting from the conditions he faced were severe enough at the time to lead those close to him to believe he might soon die. His experience at *La Princesa* in the 1950s was significantly worse. In fact, even before he was taken to *La Princesa* on November 13, 1950, his health had already been seriously impacted.[39]

During this brief period following his arrest, Don Pedro was kept in police headquarters in a room that served as an archive. This room had reinforced concrete walls, no windows, toilet, water, or electricity, and no ventilation besides whatever came through the iron door that was the room's entrance. Given food for only the first few days, in this room Don Pedro developed a nosebleed and suffered a heart attack.

Once transferred to *La Princesa*, Don Pedro was kept in solitary confinement in a cell without ventilation and without access to lawyers or visitation rights. Finally able to write letters to prison officials six months later, on May 10 Don Pedro informed them of the presence of projections of light in his cell. He stated that these light rays were causing burns on his body and that they constituted radiation attacks conducted against him by the U.S. military. After prison officials sent a doctor to examine him, Don Pedro was transferred to a cell with slightly better ventilation on May 18, 1951.

The first attack, according to Don Pedro, took place on February 18, 1951, and caused him to fall unconscious for the first time in his life. Over the next three years, Don Pedro claimed he was regularly subjected to these rays of light emanating from the walls of his cell. Whenever they appeared, after only a few minutes he noticed swelling in the parts of his body where the rays seemed to be focused—his legs, feet, arms, hands, stomach, head, neck, ears, and even his private parts. Sometimes the rays were invisible, though he could still feel their burns. These attacks caused Don Pedro to suffer from sores all over his body, severe headaches, fevers, high blood pressure, infections, and even visual impairment. By the time he was allowed to receive visits, Don Pedro had to be assisted walking down the stairs and could barely walk.

According to Don Pedro, when his cell was changed the warden of the prison said, "The bad thing about this is that I have nowhere to put him, as they have the entire prison building under radar control and they will locate him wherever he is."

Don Pedro's feeling was that he was being targeted by the U.S. government, and that they were using this method to produce a heart attack, stroke, or a death "that can be alleged is from the heart or a brain hemorrhage resulting in hemiplegia (paralysis)." He felt that by subjecting him to this unbelievable attack by radiation, his resulting death could be argued to be due to the complication of health issues rather than the assassination that it was. FBI agents kept detailed notes on everything and sent regular reports to their director.

Response To Don Pedro's Experiences

Having studied chemistry and physics in the University of Vermont and Harvard, Don Pedro called what he was experiencing both "atomic attacks" and "nuclear attacks." The only remedy available to Don Pedro, which he developed himself, was wrapping his head and body in cold, wet towels and sheets, surrounding himself with bottles of water, and keeping the floor covered with water when possible. He explained: "It is a scientific affirmation that if an atomic bomb falls while it is raining, when it falls it loses fifty percent effectiveness, because radioactivity goes down." Prison officials, on the other hand, offered only a dose of the barbiturate Seconal sodium to help him sleep. Refusing to take the drug because it affected his memory and left him physically disabled, Don Pedro said, "It is better to be burned alive than to be an idiot."

Even though FBI reports to Director J. Edgar Hoover detailed all of the symptoms Don Pedro was experiencing, one time saying, "he might not recover from his present illness," the series of doctors and psychiatrists sent by prison officials ignored all of these symptoms in their reports. Instead, everything they documented centered on the portrayal of Don Pedro as insane. They wrote about him suffering from "psychosis," "paranoia," "hallucinations," "delusions of grandeur," and the like. It was these reports the FBI then distributed widely within the U.S. government and military, controlling the narrative that the U.S. would go on to provide the press and, through them, the world.

The Puerto Rican newspaper *El Imparcial*, among others, began to print regular articles detailing the state of Don Pedro's delicate and declining health. Publications in Mexico, Cuba, and other countries also began to focus on his condition. In Argentina, one magazine published an article with the headline "The Atomic Lynching of a Martyr for Liberty," stating very clearly that Don Pedro was "slowly being murdered in jail by means of electronic rays."

The Cuban House of Representatives, on May 28, 1951, even passed a resolution that called for his release and transfer to Cuba for treatment, "taking into consideration the very grave state of the Puerto Rican patriot Dr. Pedro Albizu Campos."

Petitions for his release were also filed on the international level. In December 1952 the Nationalist Party filed a petition in both the UN and Organization of American States (OAS). On February 25, 1953, the Writer's Congress of José Martí, during their commemoration of the 100th anniversary of the birth of the Cuban patriot, wrote a letter to U.S. President Eisenhower calling for the release of Don Pedro and all other nationalists. The letter had the signatures of twenty-eight prominent individuals spanning eleven countries. The U.S. government ignored all of these pleas for Don Pedro's release and never increased the amount of medical treatment he received during this entire time.

Of course, for Don Pedro, the approach of sending medical doctors to examine him was missing the point entirely, and the use of psychiatrists was clearly tied to efforts at labeling him a madman. Rather than medical examinations, Don Pedro repeatedly called for experts in nuclear physics to investigate what was being done to him. He repeatedly refused examinations by doctors and made clear that they were not appropriate for the matter as he understood it.

Total Body Irradiation (TBI)

When the Nationalist Party petitioned the UN and OAS in 1952 in defense of Don Pedro, they also consulted and received testimony from Dr. Frédéric Joliot-Curie, France's first High Commissioner of Atomic Energy in 1945 and the recipient in 1935 of the Nobel Prize in Chemistry for the discovery of "artificial radioactivity."[40] What Dr. Joliot-Curie's testimony affirmed was that the technology for "total body irradiation" not only existed, but the attacks Don Pedro claimed to be victim of were possible.

A few years later, in 1957, the rays of light that Don Pedro described finally received a formal name in the scientific community when Columbia

University graduate student Gordon Gould coined the term LASER, an acronym standing for Light Amplification by Stimulated Emission of Radiation.[41]

When Don Pedro was briefly released from prison at the end of 1953,[42] Dr. Orlando Daumy, the president of the Cuban Cancer Association and an expert on radiation, was able to travel to Puerto Rico and examine him. He concluded that the sores on Don Pedro's body and his other symptoms were the result of exposure to intense radiation, and the effects of the radiation were weakened by the wet towels he wrapped himself with.

While Don Pedro's allegation that he was targeted with radiation attacks by the U.S. military has not been officially confirmed, revelations many years later all seem to suggest this was the case. The biggest revelation came in August 1995 when the U.S. Department of Energy confirmed that, from 1944-1974, as many as 20,000 people, including people in prison, were subjected to federally funded radiation experiments conducted by doctors, scientists, and military officials.

In a section titled 'The Case for Albizu' in his book *War Against All Puerto Ricans*, author Nelson A. Denis highlights two points that strongly suggest the possibility "that Albizu endured TBI for five years." First, he notes the visit of Dr. Marshall Brucer to Puerto Rico in February and March of 1951, the same time period when Don Pedro first reported the radiation attacks. Dr. Brucer was the medical division director of the Oak Ridge Institute of Nuclear Studies (ORINS), the same institution that built and operated some of the first TBI chambers. ORINS also received funding from the U.S. Army and the National Aeronautics and Space Administration (NASA) to study the effects of radiation on human subjects, in addition to conducting the first radiological warfare field tests for the U.S. Department of Defense.[43]

Second, he points out a multi-million-dollar contract awarded to the Sloan-Kettering Institute in the early 1950s by the Special Weapons Agency of the U.S. Department of Defense for a project studying "Post-Irradiation Syndrome on Humans." The director of the Sloan-Kettering Institute at the time, who was also a consultant for the U.S. Atomic Energy Commission, was none other than Dr. Cornelius P. Rhoads. As Denis points out, "Albizu had hounded Rhoads out of Puerto Rico [in 1932], after Rhoads wrote an infamous letter about 'killing eight Puerto Ricans' and 'transplanting cancer into several more.'" A report summarizing the project stated patients "received total body irradiation" at levels 800 percent higher than what the U.S. Nuclear Regulatory Commission identifies as being fatal without medical treatment.

As Denis wrote in his book, "A great deal of evidence, both direct and circumstantial, supports Albizu Campos' claim that he was subjected to TBI." Pedro Aponte Vázquez, a researcher on this topic, provided an in-depth presentation of all this evidence in August 1984 in front of the UN Decolonization Committee. His presentation went on to be published in 1985 and updated with additional research in 2004 as *¡Yo Acuso! Y Lo Que Pasó Después*.[44]

Many continue to seek definitive answers and accountability with respect to what Don Pedro endured. In an article published in the *Puerto Rico Herald* on April 9, 2000, New York Senator José Serrano raised the issue, writing, "Did the FBI play any role in torturing the leader of the independence movement, Dr. Pedro Albizu Campos, while he was in federal prison? The rumor persists among people in the Puerto Rican government, and elsewhere, that the FBI participated with federal prison officials in torturing Albizu Campos."

Chapter 33: 5-Month Prison Release

The Conditional Pardon Of Muñoz Marín

By the time Don Pedro was convicted and sentenced in court in August 1951, he had already undergone six months of radiation torture. Two entire years later, on September 21, 1953, journalist Teófilo Maldonado published an article reporting the critical state of the nationalist leader's health. The following week, on September 30, Governor Muñoz Marín issued a pardon resulting in Don Pedro's release from prison.

Implying the pardon was not connected to the article, Muñoz Marín claimed to have been influenced by a request sent in a letter by his friend, President José Figueres of Costa Rica. Years later, in 1979, journalist William J. Dorvillier revealed that Muñoz Marín lied about this letter from President Figueres and had in fact fabricated it himself. Aiding him in this was Arturo Morales Carrión; José Trías Monge, then-president of the Supreme Court of Puerto Rico; and Jorge Font Saldaña, a founder of the Popular Democratic Party.[45]

Presented with the text of the pardon in the warden's office, Don Pedro rejected it on the following grounds:

> *"[I]t does not include each and every one of my peers... The freedom of Albizu Campos and his life interest all free men in the world and I fully understand this pardon, but more than Albizu's life, we are all interested in the posterity of the Homeland."*

The pardon already in effect, he was forced to leave *La Princesa*. In a press conference the same day as his release, Don Pedro criticized the conditional nature of his pardon, saying, "It would be an outrage to law if the despots had to determine the way in which the subjugated peoples should fight for their freedom." Muñoz Marín, giving his own interpretation of the conditions Don Pedro criticized, said they were that he refrains from "the terrorism of a handful of fanatics against the free decisions of the people of Puerto Rico at the polls."

Don Pedro's Five Month Release From Prison

In that first press conference following his release, Don Pedro showed reporters the burns and swelling on his legs and allowed them to take photographs. He also affirmed his intent to continue working towards the independence of Puerto Rico once he regained his health. The next day Don Pedro asked Doris Torresola to raise the Puerto Rican flag outside of his home, the same flag lowered from that very spot following their arrest in 1950.[46] With the press present to witness the defiant act, Don Pedro not only spoke to them about raising a flag with the intent of never lowering it, but he also made a significant statement about an aspect of his imprisonment that continued in his own home:

"I was hoping that being home would end the efforts to burn me alive, but that has not been the case, because the electronic attacks continue as part of the plan to eliminate me."

A month later on October 30, 1953, three years after the Nationalist Insurrection of 1950, Don Pedro proclaimed:

"We have gone through atomic fire, and through all the electronic tortures the science of the United States has been able to produce... Everything that has happened is good, because the country needs to be sure that it has children who go through fire to maintain its independence."

Writing an article about the colonial nature of the Commonwealth government published in Costa Rica on January 20, 1954, Don Pedro made sure to point out that the radiation attacks were also conducted against other nationalists.[47] In the article he points to U.S. President Eisenhower as being responsible for these attacks:

> "*[T]he armed forces of that country cannot utilize atomic weapons against any enemy of the United States without the express order of the Commander-In-Chief of those armed forces.*"

As documented in a government report of information provided by an informant, on February 15, 1954, Don Pedro said the rays had turned his home into "a bonfire." A few months before, the nationalists Doris Torresola, Carmen Pérez, and Isabel Rosado brought a Geiger counter, an instrument measuring radiation levels, to his home. It registered four to nine clicks per minute when they entered, fourteen clicks when close to Don Pedro, and then broke when pressed to his body.[48]

Despite the attacks, which by this point had been going on for three years, Don Pedro was able to gain some strength and was walking better, though he still suffered from swelling and bruising. From the moment he left prison surveillance by government agents was constant and detailed records were kept on visits people made to his home.

The Attack On Congress And Final Arrest Of Don Pedro

Even with around-the-clock surveillance of Don Pedro and others in the Nationalist Party, a group of four nationalists led a completely unexpected attack inside the chamber of the U.S. Congress on March 1, 1954. The armed attack coincided with the opening day of the Tenth Inter-American Conference of the Organization of American States, an international organization the Party had been active within since its founding. Lolita Lebrón, who was living in New York as the U.S. delegate of the Nationalist Party, led Rafael Cancel Miranda, Andrés Figueroa Cordero, and Irvin Flores in the attack, which wounded five congressmen. Lebrón carried in her purse a note stating, "Before God and the world, my blood clamors for the independence of Puerto Rico! I give my life for the freedom of my homeland. This is a cry of victory in the struggle for independence." Years later, Lebrón revealed that the idea for the action originated with Don Pedro.

When news of the attack and the arrest of the four nationalists made international headlines later that day, Don Pedro was immediately informed. As day began turning to night, the journalist Teófilo Maldonado arrived hoping to interview Don Pedro. Having developed a cordial relationship with him in the preceding months, Don Pedro agreed to give Maldonado a statement under the condition that it was printed in full without edits. Methodically dictating his statement, Don Pedro validated the event calling it a "journey of sublime heroism," explaining that "The Congress of the United States is the body responsible for the military intervention of the United States in Puerto Rico for more than 50 years." According to Maldonado, with Don Pedro was Doris Torresola, Carmen Pérez, Isabel Rosado, and José Rivera Sotomayor.

Maldonado returned to Don Pedro's house on March 5 to inform him of the impending cancellation of his pardon in addition to the preparation of the local police, National Guard, FBI, and others, for a siege on his home. The response Maldonado received was:

> *"We will not provoke anyone, but if we are provoked we will answer the provocation. We are in our home and in our right as Puerto Ricans. We have not committed any crime."*

As night fell, the police and military, equipped with protective vests and machine guns, began situating themselves within the streets and adjacent homes. The following morning, they received the arrest order for Don

Pedro from Governor Muñoz Marín for violation of the terms of his conditional release. As agents began knocking on his door at 6AM, and then tried to force their entry, Don Pedro opened fire with a revolver.

According to police reports, during the half hour shootout all the nationalists inside returned fire. After a pause in the exchange, tear gas was thrown into the house. Soon after the smoke achieved its desired effect, José Rivera Sotomayor came out of the house first. He hoped that by coming out first he could draw fire towards himself and increase the chance of Don Pedro being able to come out after him without being immediately killed. Carmen Pérez came out next, telling authorities that Don Pedro was lying unconscious on the floor.

Passed out from the gas, Doris Torresola and Isabel Rosado were carried out of the home, and then, finally, Don Pedro was carried out last. With Don Pedro semi-conscious, journalist Teófilo Maldonado, who had been present for the siege and arrest, approached him to ask if he had anything to say. Don Pedro mumbled "We have done our duty."

Immediately, the nationalists were taken by ambulance to prison, Don Pedro to the State Penitentiary in Río Piedras, also known as *Oso Blanco*, and the female nationalists to the women's prison in Vega Alta. The second and final period of Don Pedro's leadership, from 1947-1954, came to a close. By the end of the following day, March 7, several high-ranking leaders of the *Partido Comunista Puertorriqueño* were arrested as well as another forty-two members of the Nationalist Party. The charges used for these arrests were violation of the Gag Law.

Notes To Chapters 26 - 33

[1] Rosado, *Las Llamas de la Aurora.*

[2] Albizu-Campos Meneses and Fr. Rodríguez León, eds., *Escritos.*

[3] Laura de Albizu Campos, *Albizu Campos y la Independencia de Puerto Rico.*

[4] For more on this law, how it affected the society in Puerto Rico, and how it was used against political dissidents, see Chapter 31.

[5] Acosta, *La Palabra Como Delito.*

[6] The developments associated with this law are discussed more in Chapters 29 and 30.

[7] Seijo Bruno, *La Insurrección Nacionalista en Puerto Rico 1950.*

[8] This chapter is based on an article I wrote titled "Pedro Albizu Campos: Speaking Truth To Power" that was published in La Respuesta magazine on 14 April 2015.

[9] Center for Puerto Rican Studies Library and Archives, *Oral History, The Ruth M. Reynolds Papers.*

[10] El Dr. Manuel de la Pila Iglesias: Ilustre médico de Ponce y Puerto Rico, Galenus Vol. 9.

[11] Seijo Bruno, *La Insurrección Nacionalista en Puerto Rico 1950.*

[12] Rosado, *Las Llamas de la Aurora.*

[13] Members of the Nationalist Party were known by a few nicknames. One was Las Camisas Negras because of their black shirts. Another was Los Decididos, the Decided Ones, because of their absolute commitment to national liberation.

[14] The Puerto Rican Independence Party (PIP) was founded in 1946 after the Popular Democratic Party definitively abandoned its support of independence for Puerto Rico. As a political party, the PIP participated in the elections.

[15] Denis, *War Against All Puerto Ricans.*

[16] Laura de Albizu Campos, *Albizu Campos y la Independencia de Puerto Rico.*

[17] It was titled "Law for the Organization of a Constitutional Government for the People of Puerto Rico."

[18] After the U.S. took control of Puerto Rico in 1898, every governor was appointed. This was true during Spanish rule as well.

[19] Albizu-Campos Meneses and Fr. Rodríguez León, eds., *Escritos.*

20 Rosado, *Las Llamas de la Aurora.*

21 Denis, *War Against All Puerto Ricans.*

22 Laura de Albizu Campos, *Albizu Campos y la Independencia de Puerto Rico.*

23 Seijo Bruno, *La Insurrección Nacionalista en Puerto Rico 1950.*

24 The New York Times, *Island Rebels Ask U.N. To Investigate.*

25 United Nations, *Chapter XI: Declaration Regarding Non-Self-Governing Territories, Charter Of The United Nations.*

26 Rosado, *Las Llamas de la Aurora.*

27 Seijo Bruno, *La Insurrección Nacionalista en Puerto Rico 1950.*

28 Denis, *War Against All Puerto Ricans.*

29 The New York Times, *Assassin's Boasts Trapped Suspects; Arrests in New York Followed Collazo Bragging, Grand Jury Witness Says.*

30 The New York Times, *Commutation Approved.*

31 Paralitici, *Sentencia Impuesta.*

32 Medina Ramírez, *El Movimiento Libertador en la Historia de Puerto Rico.*

33 Laura de Albizu Campos, *Albizu Campos y la Independencia de Puerto Rico.*

34 Acosta, *La Palabra Como Delito.*

35 Acosta, *La Palabra Como Delito.*

36 *El Mundo, El Imparcial, El Día,* and *El Universal.*

37 Rosado, *Las Llamas de la Aurora.*

38 Acosta Lespier, *La Mordaza (The Gag Law).*

39 Rosado, *Las Llamas de la Aurora.*

40 Encyclopædia Britannica, *Frédéric and Irène Joliot-Curie: French Chemists.*

41 American Institute of Physics, *Bright Idea: The First Lasers.*

42 More on this brief release from prison in the next chapter.

43 Denis, *War Against All Puerto Ricans.*

44 Aponte Vázquez, *¡Yo Acuso!.*

45 Aponte Vázquez, *Locura Por Decreto.*

46 Rosado, *Las Llamas de la Aurora.*

---

[47] Albizu-Campos Meneses and Fr. Rodríguez León, eds., *Escritos*.

[48] Denis, *War Against All Puerto Ricans*.

Seventh Period — Final Years and Legacy

Chapter 34: Final Prison Term

The Final Imprisonment Of Don Pedro

As far as reasons given to the media for revoking Don Pedro's pardon, *El Imparcial* published statements given by both Muñoz Marín and Chief of Police Salvador T. Roig on March 8, 1954. According to Muñoz Marín, the reason was the ordering of the attack on the U.S. Congress. According to Roig, however, the reason was the interview Don Pedro gave to journalist Teófilo Maldonado that was published unedited in *El Imparcial*. Whatever the reason, many lawyers spoke very strongly against the revocation of the pardon on completely different grounds: the revocation order was signed only by Muñoz Marín, violating the constitutional requirement that it also be signed by a judge or court officer before any arrest.

The trials for those who had been with Don Pedro during the March 6 raid on his home took place over ten days in May 1955.[1] Legal efforts on Don Pedro's behalf included Francisco Hernández Vargas bringing to the Supreme Court of Puerto Rico the argument that Muñoz Marín had not received the required additional signatures needed to revoke Don Pedro's pardon; African American lawyer Conrad Lynn bringing the same argument to U.S. Federal Court; and Jorge Luis Landing again taking the case to the Supreme Court of Puerto Rico in the beginning of 1957. All efforts were opposed in the courts. Conrad Lynn's effort was not even entertained by the U.S. federal court on the grounds of "not having exhausted all the resources in the courts of the country."

Arriving in prison with a delicate state of health, Don Pedro's condition continued to worsen. Having to be hospitalized more than once during this prison term, the level of security at the hospital was no better than the actual prison. Security was so strong that police were pressured into giving the press an explanation. Captain Gerardo Delgado said, "Albizu's room in the Presbyterian [Hospital] is considered an extension of the penitentiary and due to the lack of sufficient penal guards to set up surveillance there, the police are cooperating in the custody."[2]

The Conclusion Of Political Torture

Don Pedro's first hospitalization during this prison term took place on March 29, 1956. Biographer Marisa Rosado outlined the events leading up to his hospitalization as such: "Hospital personnel, following instructions from the secretary of justice, José Trías Monge, referred all calls from the press and the public to his office, promising to call the doctors to provide rigorous information. It was then that Dr. Rafael Troyano de los Ríos confirmed the news that Albizu had suffered a cerebral thrombosis. He explained that on Monday he had woken up with his right hand paralyzed, on Tuesday with his right leg and that he was developing paralysis throughout that side. On Wednesday morning he noticed that he had difficulty speaking and drowsiness, and he remained like this until Thursday March 29, the night he was hospitalized."

While this account from the doctor begins on Monday March 26, the press had published news of Don Pedro suffering a stroke on Sunday March 25, a full five days before he was transferred to the Presbyterian Hospital in Santurce for care.

After being transferred back to a clinic in the prison a few months later, on June 15, and despite his difficulty speaking, Don Pedro informed a visiting doctor on August 29 that he was still being attacked by "nuclear rays." On November 9 he suffered a relapse and was brought again to the Presbyterian Hospital. From this point on Don Pedro was paralyzed on the right side of his body and unable to speak for the rest of his life.

The political torture of Don Pedro had reached its conclusion short of death, and, as author Nelson Denis put it, "Albizu Campos had been silenced forever."[3] In July 1959 he developed jaundice as a result of hepatitis. In March 1960 he was denied parole despite a doctor strongly urging a conditional release in order to receive better treatment for his critical state. In September 1964 a group of lawyers visited Don Pedro, still in the Presbyterian Hospital, to gain his permission in filing a second habeas corpus petition in pursuit of his release. No matter how close they got to Don Pedro, they could not hear him when he appeared to try speaking, and when they wrote on a piece of paper and presented it to him, they were unable to see or hear any clear reaction.

Political efforts to silence Don Pedro were combined with the repression faced by his family and those close to him. The editor of *El Imparcial* and former president of the Nationalist Party, Antonio Ayuso Valdivieso, was turned away when trying to visit Don Pedro. Father Martín Bernstein, a close friend of Don Pedro who had hoped to give him the final Catholic sacrament of the last rites, was also turned away. Ana María Campos, Don Pedro's cousin born to his Aunt Rosa, also had challenges in visiting him even though she at one point had visitation permission. Officials also gave Don Pedro's son, Pedro Albizu Meneses, issues entering and remaining in Puerto Rico from Cuba. His wife, Doña Laura, was outright denied a visa to travel to see him from her residence in Mexico.

International Outcry And Final Release

From the beginning of his imprisonment countless people throughout the world protested the situation of Don Pedro, including the press which published updates regarding his health. The Cuban Federation of University Students wrote a statement representing 18,000 students holding the U.S. government responsible for Don Pedro's condition, asking the UN to investigate his "political murder." Upon completing the minimum length of his sentence on March 9, 1957, there was a significant effort to get him released. Despite these continued pleas for the release of Don Pedro, nothing happened until December 30, 1959, when Muñoz Marín issued a pardon ending his sentence for violation of the Gag Law. Not changing anything about Don Pedro's imprisonment, the pardon did not actually result in his release since it did not cover other charges he was also convicted and sentenced for.

In commemoration of his 70th birthday in September 1961, a protest was organized in front of the Presbyterian Hospital that lasted for days. Simultaneous protests were held elsewhere in Latin America, the Caribbean, Europe, and Asia. As a conclusion to the days of protest, a march to his home where he was arrested took place on September 12, ending with the reading of a proclamation declaring people of the world in favor of the liberation of Don Pedro and all other Puerto Rican nationalists, and of the independence of Puerto Rico.

The year 1964 saw the governments of Argentina, Chile, Brazil, and Spain write directly to Governor Muñoz Marín seeking the release of Don Pedro. Each of these governments feared and wanted to avoid the death of Don Pedro in prison. With Don Pedro's condition at its absolute worse, and Muñoz Marín about to be replaced as governor, the winner of the November 3, 1964 election, Roberto Sánchez Vilella, is said to have told Muñoz Marín the following: "You put him in jail, and if I were you, for history, I would release him before leaving the governorship, because I warn you, if you don't pardon him, I will pardon him."

On November 15, 1964, after ten years either in prison or hospitalized under strict police custody, Don Pedro was issued a full pardon by Muñoz Marín and freed. Over the period from 1936 to his final release in 1964, a span of 28 years, Don Pedro spent a total of about 24 years in prison, in exile, or hospitalized.[4]

Chapter 35: Final Months And Funeral

Becoming A Living Legend

When Don Pedro was pardoned by Governor Muñoz Marín on November 15, 1964, he had been in the Presbyterian Hospital since 1956. His pardon produced a great reaction throughout Puerto Rico and many people made their way to the hospital to witness his release from custody. By this point in his life, Don Pedro had earned space for himself in the history of Puerto Rico as a symbol of its fight for liberation from colonialism. Juan Antonio Corretjer later wrote about him as being among those people who "by the strength of soul, passes to posterity still alive."

One month later, on December 12, 1964, the Argentinian revolutionary Ernesto 'Ché' Guevara dedicated part of his speech in front of the United Nations General Assembly to highlight the case of Don Pedro: "We express our solidarity with the people of Puerto Rico and their great leader, Pedro Albizu Campos, who, in another act of hypocrisy, was released at age 72, almost unable to speak, paralyzed, after spending a lifetime in jail. Albizu Campos is a symbol of the as yet unfree but indomitable Latin America. Years and years in prison, almost unbearable pressures in jail, mental torture, solitude, total isolation from his people and his family, the insolence of the conqueror and his lackeys in the land where he was born—nothing broke his will. The delegation of Cuba, on behalf of its people, pays a tribute of admiration and gratitude to a patriot who dignifies our America."

The Declining Condition Of Don Pedro

According to information provided to the FBI by an informant on November 17, 1964 regarding Don Pedro's condition, the revolutionary leader once well-known as a captivating orator left the hospital hardly able to speak at an audible volume, and had a vocabulary limited to about ten words. It also appeared that "he could not concentrate enough to understand the meaning of spoken or written words."[5]

Once released from the hospital, Don Pedro was taken to a residence in Hato Rey owned by Dr. Virginio Rodríguez Marrero who would be one of the doctors, along with Dr. Ricardo Cordero and Dr. Luis Cuello, in charge of his care. He received support from countless other people, including friends, students, and associates in the political arena, all who helped cater to his needs or simply kept him company. A nurse named Conchita Santos de Marks and a longtime nationalist and friend of Don Pedro's, Juanita Ojeda Maldonado, are also known to have provided daily care.

Don Pedro's daughter Laura, who had not seen him since 1950, was able to make her way to Puerto Rico from Peru in December 1964 with her four daughters. His wife Doña Laura, who had been in New York City since 1960 working in the UN as a representative of the Cuban government, was finally able to get a diplomatic visa approved and travel to Puerto Rico on April 9, 1965. Don Pedro's children Rosa and Pedro, however, were not allowed by immigration officials to enter Puerto Rico. During this time Don Pedro's health did not improve and his body began to stop functioning normally.

In February 1965 Don Pedro was recorded with a 104-degree fever, a viral respiratory infection, and uremic poisoning indicating his kidneys were not filtering toxins out of his body. In the month of April his condition began its final descent: on the 14th his paralysis began to affect his throat, making it difficult to swallow; on the 16th water filled his lungs, and inflammation in his face and throat made him unable to move his lips and jaw; on the 17th he was confirmed to have pneumonia and kidney failure; on the morning of the 19th his doctor said he was unconscious, his kidneys had stopped functioning, his throat was blocked due to the inflammation, and he had a 100 degree fever. At 7:30AM that day a priest performed the Catholic sacrament of the last rites and those close to him began organizing his funeral. Two days later, at 9:40PM on April 21, Don Pedro was pronounced deceased.

The Funeral And Recognition Of A Patriot

Taken to Jensen Funeral Home in Santurce, the body of Don Pedro was prepared for presentation over the course of more than 15 hours and was embalmed with a preservative used for the first time in Puerto Rico that the funeral home's owner told the media meant, "Albizu's body will remain intact for the next 100 years."

The sculptor Francisco Vázquez Díaz also made a bust of his face, known as a death mask, and his hands. Once fully prepared, Don Pedro's body was displayed in the funeral home for two days until he was carried in his casket, draped with the Puerto Rican flag that had been raised outside his home in the 1950s, to the *Ateneo Puertorriqueño* where he was displayed for one day.[6]

During this entire time an honor guard composed of six people per shift was maintained. University students also displayed a giant banner with Don Pedro's image and raised the Puerto Rican flag to half-mast on the University of Puerto Rico campus in his honor.

After he passed and had been placed inside his casket, Don Pedro's wife Doña Laura said the following: "Albizu Campos lived for his people and for them he died in the sacrifice imposed by the enemy of freedom and the independence of his homeland. Lives devoted to a cause like the one he served transcend death. His example illuminates the future and the memory of him grows until it reaches an unsurpassed stature. Puerto Rico will reach the goal set by him and the recognition of his people will be the pedestal of his glory."

The death of Don Pedro was a significant event in Puerto Rico. People from all facets of society set aside the many differences they might have had and united in paying tribute to the revolutionary leader—elders, children, nationalists, communists, socialists, statehood supporters, masons, students, union workers, feminists, artists, poets, lawyers, etc. Don Pedro was also recognized in meetings and motions of the Puerto Rican Senate and House of Representatives. The reaction went beyond Puerto Rico and into cities of the U.S. and other countries internationally.

Many people from these places made the trip to attend his services in Puerto Rico. The Venezuelan government, who had a representative present for the burial, observed five minutes of silence in a parliamentary meeting. Hundreds of condolence cards were also sent to Don Pedro's family from around the world.

While he wanted to be buried in the town of his birth, Sector Tenerías in Ponce, Don Pedro's wife made the decision to have him buried in Old San Juan. Becoming one of the largest processions in Puerto Rican history, over 100,000 people followed the casket of Don Pedro in the march from the *Ateneo Puertorriqueño* to the Santa María Magdalena de Pazzis Cemetery. On the way to the cemetery the procession stopped at the Church of San José where a short ceremony was held in his honor. Earth from Tenerías was brought to his burial and poured over his coffin.

At the burial, Catholic priest and activist Víctor Margarito Santiago Arce, known as Father Margarito, shared these words: "We must honor Albizu Campos who manifested the repudiation of the humiliation our people suffer... Don Pedro has not died and will never die. The mourning must be celebrated in Puerto Rico for many people who are morally dead."

Chapter 36: The Patriotic Struggle Of Don Pedro

Unwavering Commitment To The Nation

When Mexican philosopher and politician José Vasconcelos visited Puerto Rico in 1926, he was immediately impressed by Don Pedro's intelligence and absolute commitment to working in defense of the oppressed. He was particularly impacted by Don Pedro's decision to turn down high-paying positions within the U.S. and Puerto Rican governments. Vasconcelos wrote the following: "I am sure that one day this ungrateful America of ours will know him and greet him as one of its heroes. He lives in defense of the poor; that is, he hardly lives. Temptation stalks him daily in the form of commissions and jobs that he rejects because it is contrary to the doctrine of collaboration with the invaders... He lives like a saint..."[7]

This willingness to disregard his personal convenience and livelihood in favor of working towards the independence of Puerto Rico is something that remained consistent throughout his life and that many highlighted in their works memorializing him after his passing in 1965.[8]

In addition to committing to the struggle for liberation in Puerto Rico at the expense of his own livelihood and comfort, Don Pedro's example of commitment holds significance in another respect. As explained by Juan Antonio Corretjer, this significance lies in Don Pedro "having been in Puerto Rico, lived in Puerto Rico, fought in Puerto Rico and died in Puerto Rico... None of our great men of the past had the privilege of living that kind of life. They had all died outside of Puerto Rico, but Albizu is the first to be born, live, fight and die in Puerto Rico, giving the great example that from Puerto Rico you don't have to leave, you have to stay here until the end." Having stated publicly that he does not believe in voluntary exile, Don Pedro lived out his commitment to Puerto Rico while being present there despite the intense surveillance and repression he faced, as well as the many threats and attempts on his life.

By Any Means Necessary

In terms of the forms of struggle used by Don Pedro, he truly exemplified the phrase 'by any means necessary.'[9] Independence activist and founder of the *Partido Socialista Puertorriqueño*, Juan Mari Brás, highlighted this fact in his 1984 book *El Independentismo en Puerto Rico: Su Pasado, Su Presente y su Porvenir.*[10] In that book, he wrote, "There is not a single one of the great and small forms of struggle tested in the history of independence that Albizu Campos had not handled at some point in his life, in his career. And the worst of it is that we have not created any new ones. All we have done is reheat Albizuist formulas, applying them to new situations, from new perspectives."

Driving the point home, Mari Brás quoted the following list written by Corretjer of the elements inherent in Don Pedro's work: "The philosophical disquisition, the legal exposition, the religious, political or agitating oration; the pamphlet, article and private correspondence, the discreet management between friends and sympathizers in the opposing field, suffrage as a means of political organization and doctrinal discussion, the boycott as resistance and revolutionary technique, the strike of workers and students, diplomatic means, international work, contacts with foreign governments and institutions at any given time available, Puerto Ricans residing abroad, mainly residing in New York, whom with his inspiration and mandate he turned into an election source that brought to Congress a representative of the independence of Puerto Rico; the great Vito Marcantonio, whose parliamentary genius turned his Puerto Rican base into a remarkable number of congressional votes; conspiracy, direct action, street fighting, insurrection..."

Today in Puerto Rico, there are still pro-independence political organizations that seek elected positions within the colonial government; pro-independence political organizations that boycott the national elections; groups that accept armed struggle as a tactic in the fight for liberation; labor unions that focus on organizing the power of workers in effecting meaningful change, through general strikes if necessary; student organizations that protest and work against harmful educational reforms, also conducting strikes if necessary; groups that work within the United Nations and other international bodies in support of decolonization; groups that promote the holding of a constitutional convention as a first step in the de-colonial process; and the list goes on. In some cases, these groups and efforts came about as products of the direct influence of Don Pedro, whose image and/or words these groups, organizations, and individuals sometimes display.

The Transfiguration Of A People

While it is true that Don Pedro adopted the Catholic religion, it is important to understand that he was also a person that genuinely contemplated profound spiritual aspects of life. He is also known for connecting these meditations to the liberation struggle.[11]

In an essay focusing on Don Pedro's 1950 statement that "the homeland is undergoing its glorious transfiguration," author Ivonne Acosta points out Don Pedro's approach of establishing as sacred symbols and rites the relics and events of Puerto Rico's revolutionary history.[12] For example, the single-starred flag of Puerto Rico was regarded as a sacred symbol of the nation, and the city of Lares was a holy ground to be honored through a yearly pilgrimage. Symbols and rites were things Don Pedro felt all national entities had, and so he began introducing them to the movement upon becoming president of the Nationalist Party in 1930.

In her essay, Acosta also highlights the following affirmation Don Pedro made at the 1936 funeral of Elias Beauchamp and Hiram Rosado:

> *"Nationalism has brought to the homeland the transmutation of its being, for man was not born to vegetate... courage is the only thing that allows the transmutation of man for higher purposes."*

She points to this as the moment when he begins tying, at least publicly, the concept of transmutation with the mission of Puerto Rican nationalism. Acosta then cites the following statement by Don Pedro from April 8, 1950 about the monument of Ramón Emeterio Betances as another example of his use of the concept of transfiguration:

> *"This monument is not only a monument, it is something that has undergone the transfiguration because that monument has within it the remains of the great patrician."*

This transmutation and transfiguration Don Pedro referred to was the emergence of the people of Puerto Rico out of the prevailing colonial mentality. It was the process of transforming from colonial subjects into human beings given historical purpose through a living connection with the revolutionary legacy of their nation's patriots. It was the primary objective of his nationalist leadership. Some have used this understanding to describe Don Pedro's brand of nationalism as a kind of liberation theology. Don Pedro commented on the need to undergo this process during a speech on October 10, 1935:

> *"Today there form characterless beings who eat each other, the total happiness of our children is destroyed; to none the truth is preached, materialism leads them to death in body and soul. We must get out of this state and make of our people a people of humans, of martyrs, of saints."*

The process of transformation was initiated by Don Pedro in large part through his use of history as a tool to raise the consciousness of the masses. Not only did he speak on history, but he provided symbols that could be seen, places that could be visited, and actions that could be performed. Don Pedro sought to elevate the national consciousness of Puerto Ricans so they could genuinely develop and embody the virtues of courage and sacrifice needed to defend their dignity and ideals. That these sacred symbols, places, and duties continue to be honored today is a testament to the significant and undeniable impact of Don Pedro's leadership, and to his understanding of the power they held.

Chapter 37: Passing The Torch Of Liberation

A Purpose Connected To History

César Andreu Iglesias, one-time president of the Puerto Rican Communist Party and co-founder of the publication *Claridad*, published an article in *El Imparcial* on April 24, 1965, three days after the transition of Don Pedro. In it he provided his own definition of what Don Pedro represented for the nation of Puerto Rico. His words speak to the profound impact Don Pedro had as the leader of a people's liberation movement: "To define Albizu Campos, one word is enough: Albizu was the conscience of Puerto Rico. He was for those who followed him. He was even more so for the many who denied him... Albizu accepted his role as an inexorable fate. Nothing so terrible as making a conscience of a people. He spoke when it was necessary to speak. He denounced when it was necessary to denounce. He accused when it was necessary to accuse. And he was always ready to face the consequences. His action did not know of compromises, concessions, returns. He acted as what he was: an unappealable, absolute conscience."[13]

Besides accepting it as fate, Don Pedro was very clear that his leadership of the Nationalist Party was connected to the longer, historic struggle for independence. He once proclaimed: "This is the continuation of the work of Betances and the founders of the Republic in Lares in 1868." In 1931, an interesting event of great symbolic significance related to this continuity took place in Santurce's Barrio Obrero.

The journalist Manuel Rivera Matos, who was also serving as the Nationalist Party's secretary general that year, conducted an interview with Don Pedro Angleró, a 110-year-old former enslaved person who took part in *El Grito de Lares*. In the interview, Don Angleró explained that he more than just knew about Ramón Emeterio Betances—Betances was the doctor of his home. Present for the interview was Don Angleró's grandnephew Ambrosio Angleró, at the time the president of the Barrio Obrero chapter of the Nationalist Party, as well as Juan Antonio Corretjer and Don Pedro. During the meeting a symbolic moment took place where Don Angleró, in his position as the only remaining survivor of *El Grito*, recognized Don Pedro as the person to carry forward the legacy of the patriots of Lares. After this meeting took place Don Angleró became sick and, less than one month later, on October 16, 1931, passed away.[14]

For the 100th anniversary of *El Grito de Lares* in 1968, the Nationalist Party highlighted this symbolic moment by publishing literature with the images of Betances, Don Angleró, and Don Pedro, and the words "Pass the torch of history and freedom."

Upholding Don Pedro's Revolutionary Legacy

Before Don Pedro passed away, he might not have had a similar moment where he passed on the torch of the struggle, but he definitely had successors that continued the work. Because of the state of his health during his final prison term from 1954-1964, organizations inspired by him were formed before he even took his final breath.

Juan Mari Brás, a pro-independence student activist in the 1940s University of Puerto Rico, formed the *Movimiento Pro-Independencia* (MPI) in 1959, which later became the Puerto Rican Socialist Party (PSP) in 1971.[15] Juan Antonio Corretjer, who worked very closely with Don Pedro in the 1930s and then became active as a communist, formed the *Liga Socialista Puertorriqueño* in 1962. As for the Nationalist Party of Puerto Rico, Jacinto Rivera Pérez, who upon Don Pedro's return from exile in 1947 had been elected its vice-president, served as the Party's president for many years after Don Pedro transitioned in 1965.

Of course, the legacy of Don Pedro cannot be discussed without also discussing armed struggle and the armed groups that developed in Puerto Rico through his influence. Just like groups mentioned previously, armed groups inspired by Don Pedro's legacy were also formed in the years before his transition, with many more developing after. In his book focusing on Filiberto Ojeda Ríos[16] and the *Movimiento Independentista Revolucionario Armado* (MIRA), author Álvaro M. Rivera Ruiz wrote that Don Pedro was "ideologically and emotionally reincarnated in this generation of combatants." Rivera Ruiz also pointed out the main difference between the strategy of the Nationalist Party and these new armed groups, writing, "the former made a direct confrontation with the regime, while the second opted for a clandestine struggle, as a security mechanism."[17] The next group formed by Ojeda Ríos, in 1976, and which continues to be active today, is the *Ejército Popular Boricua-Macheteros*.

Just like Don Pedro, members of these armed groups also faced prison terms for seditious conspiracy. As an example, the *Fuerzas Armadas de Liberación Nacional* (FALN), a group based in the U.S. that emerged in 1974, had fourteen members arrested and charged with seditious conspiracy between 1980 and 1983.[18] Most of these FALN members were released in 1999, after serving 16-19 years in prison, when U.S. President Bill Clinton granted them clemency. Oscar López Rivera was the last to be released, his sentence being commuted by U.S. President Barack Obama in 2017 after he had served 36 years in prison.

An important organization to emerge that was greatly influenced by Don Pedro was the Young Lords, a Chicago street organization that became political in 1968. They went on to have a national impact and a significant presence in New York City. The Young Lords, taking inspiration from the Black Panther Party, adopted a militant activist approach and ran several community service programs that organized free breakfast for children, clothing donations for those in need, rehabilitation for drug addiction, child care, street clean-ups, political education, health testing, and more.

Within both their political education classes and the articles printed in their newspaper, the Young Lords frequently highlighted Don Pedro's life and legacy in addition to others like Ramón Emeterio Betances and *El Grito de Lares*, Blanca Canales and the Nationalist Insurrection of 1950, and Lolita Lebrón and the 1954 attack on congress. Central to the Young Lords' struggle, and appearing as the first of their thirteen-point organizational program, was self-determination for Puerto Ricans— "liberation on the island and inside the United States."[19]

Chapter 38: Dr. Laura Meneses de Albizu Campos

A Pioneer From Peru

Dr. Laura Meneses del Carpio was born in Arequipa, Peru on March 31, 1894. The youngest of three children, her father Juan Rosa Meneses del Pino was a Colonel in the Peruvian Army. Due to her father's position in the military, Doña Laura traveled frequently. And due to the importance her parents placed on education, her father eventually took a position near the capital of Lima so that Doña Laura could attend the *Universidad Nacional Mayor de San Marcos*, which she entered in 1911.[20]

Already having a stellar academic background, she became the first woman to qualify for a distinguished honor award in a tie with another incoming male student. With university-educated women being a recent reality that was still the target of active male opposition, the award, which included a grant, was given to the male candidate.

In 1913, Doña Laura completed a bachelor's degree and, in 1918, a doctorate degree, both in Natural Sciences.[21] Born with a passion for music, she also graduated from a training she had been attending as a pianist. Although her piano instructor urged her to continue her studies in music rather than science, even writing letters of recommendation to U.S. music schools for her, Doña Laura decided to continue her education in the natural sciences and became the first Latin American woman to study in Harvard University.

When she entered Harvard's female section of Radcliffe College, she was fluent in Spanish, English, and two indigenous languages of Peru, Quechua and Aymara. Because of her ancestry she also had a well-formed identity that went deeper than a Latin American perspective to include an

Indigenous point of reference.[22] Although enrolled in Radcliffe College, Doña Laura was allowed to attend classes in Harvard's male campus since she already had such a high level of education. During her time in Harvard, she took twelve courses, earning an A in eleven and an A- in one.

One night, when attending an event organized by students to host the Indian poet Rabindranath Tagore, she met Don Pedro for the first time, mistaking him for someone of Indian descent due to his physical features. Formally introduced to him during a dinner not long after, they immediately began dating and establishing the relationship that lasted the rest of their lives. Doña Laura's decision to move to Puerto Rico with Don Pedro dramatically changed the course of her life.

Living In Full Commitment To Liberation

When Doña Laura married Don Pedro in July 1922, because of the laws existing at the time in her home country, she lost her Peruvian citizenship and gained the U.S. citizenship her husband himself had received just a few years before in 1917.[23] In deciding to move to Puerto Rico, she also made the decision to abandon her professional career. As her presence became known in Puerto Rico, Doña Laura was offered positions as a university professor that she declined on the principle of refusing to work within the colonial regime.[24] In a 1957 letter to her daughter Laura Esperanza, Doña Laura said the following about how her life changed following her marriage to Don Pedro:

> *"Since I got married I have lived in that world that, in order not to become a mirage, demands the continuous oblation[25] of our personality. For this I had to give up my most basic needs, my whims, my desires, my concerns. The only thing I did not renounce was my joy because I was next to your father whose greatness highlighted the superficiality of all things."*

Carrying and birthing two of Don Pedro's children, Doña Laura was pregnant with their third when Don Pedro had to leave for his political tour of Latin America in 1927. To support his trip, Doña Laura agreed to sell all their furniture to raise the needed funds, and to take their children and live with her family in Peru for the duration of the trip.

After the family moved back to Puerto Rico together in 1930, Doña Laura returned to Peru in 1933 for a year in order to recover from a health condition she was battling. In that year she also served as the foreign delegate of the Nationalist Party in her first of many political roles at the international level.[26]

After Don Pedro and the other nationalists were sent to Atlanta Penitentiary in 1937, Doña Laura went on to play a significant role in the campaign to secure their release. In 1938 she moved to New York City where she not only influenced the founding of an organization in support of the political prisoners—made up of elements from the American Civil Liberties Union and other groups—but she also influenced the founding of a similar group based in Mexico.[27] In July of that year, she made the only trip to visit her husband in Atlanta Penitentiary that she was allowed—her countless other requests to visit him were denied. In 1939, she moved to Cuba and helped found yet another organization in support of the release of Don Pedro and the nationalists. Throughout her work with the campaign for the release of the nationalists, Doña Laura maintained a clear and consistent call for Puerto Rico's independence.

In 1941, Doña Laura moved, at the insistence of her husband, to her family's home in Lima, Peru with her children. From there she continued her work connected to Puerto Rico, maintaining a consistent correspondence with many leaders. Included among her frequent contacts were leaders within the American Civil Liberties Union, which played a significant role in relaying information they obtained from Atlanta Penitentiary prison officials to both Doña Laura and politicians in Washington, D.C.

During this period in Peru Doña Laura lived a very humble life where money was very difficult to obtain. For much of this time she wove sweaters that her counterpart Juan Juarbe, a devoted nationalist that was her living partner for many years, would sell. In these years following 1937, Doña Laura distinguished herself as a leader of international advocacy work related to the release of the nationalists in prison and independence for Puerto Rico.

An International Legacy

When Doña Laura finally returned to Puerto Rico in April 1948 to be with her husband, she was informed that her U.S. citizenship was revoked and that she was not a recognized citizen of any country. In May 1950, colonial repression in Puerto Rico reached a level that forced her to move to and center her work once again in Cuba. Doña Laura's activism not only continued for the next two decades, up to her physical death on April 15, 1973, but it actually increased. The colonial narrative of the Commonwealth government, which was being put in place in a very careful and strategic way, placed a heightened importance on providing information on Puerto Rico at the international level that countered the biased and misleading reports provided by the U.S. and/or colonial government. Doña Laura played a tremendous role in supporting and organizing these efforts.

Following the March 1954 attack on congress, Doña Laura was targeted by the Cuban regime of dictator Fulgencio Batista and was forced to make her way to Mexico, where she continued her work. In Mexico by April, her residence became a meeting place for activists and revolutionaries from many countries. Most notably, she was frequently visited by Fidel Castro, Ernesto 'Ché' Guevara, and others of the Cuban 26th of July Movement. At one point, all the movement's writings were given to Doña Laura for editing before they were publicized. After the successful overthrow of the Batista regime in 1959, Doña Laura immediately moved back to Cuba to support the revolutionary changes taking place there.

With Cuba as a secure base of support, Doña Laura continued her international advocacy for the independence of Puerto Rico and the release of her husband, still in prison and in worse health than ever. In November 1959, she attended an international congress in Chile, afterwards making her way to a few other South American countries. In March 1960, she attended the 50th anniversary of International Women's Day in Copenhagen. From there she visited China, where she was able to meet and speak with Mao Tse Tung, and then Paris and Madrid.

After returning to Cuba, she was granted, on January 18, 1961, Cuban citizenship in addition to becoming an official delegate for Cuba within the United Nations. From that year until 1966 she sat in all meetings of the UN General Assembly in New York City and spoke as the official representative of the Republic of Cuba.

Doña Laura was able to be present for the physical death of her husband, and his funeral. She never stopped working in support of Puerto Rico's independence. She led in the formation of several organizations, spoke at international congresses, directly supported revolutionary movements, and much more. Doña Laura's own physical death at 79 years of age in 1973 was the result of a ruptured brain aneurysm. Amazingly, doctors noted their surprise that she had lived so long because her brain aneurysm was congenital, a condition present at birth usually resulting in a lifespan of about 20 years. Her body was interred in the Colón Cemetery of Havana, Cuba the following day on April 16.

Notes To Chapters 34 - 38

[1] Medina Ramírez, *El Movimiento Libertador en la Historia de Puerto Rico.*

[2] Rosado, *Las Llamas de la Aurora.*

[3] Denis, *War Against All Puerto Ricans.*

[4] Paralitici, *Sentencia Impuesta.*

[5] Aponte Vázquez, *Los Últimos Días De Don Pedro Albizu Campos.*

[6] Rosado, *Las Llamas de la Aurora.*

[7] Rosado, *Las Llamas de la Aurora.*

[8] Laura de Albizu Campos, *Albizu Campos y la Independencia de Puerto Rico.*

[9] This phrase was made popular by Malcolm X, the black revolutionary leader assassinated on April 21, 1965, exactly three months after Don Pedro's passing.

[10] Mari Brás, *El Independentismo En Puerto Rico.*

[11] Meneses Albizu-Campos, *La Espiritualidad de Pedro Albizu Campos.*

[12] Acosta Lespier, *La "Transfiguración Gloriosa De La Patria" De Acuerdo A Pedro Albizu Campos.*

[13] Rosado, *Las Llamas de la Aurora.*

[14] Partido Nacionalista De Puerto Rico, *Plantao En La Revolución.*

[15] Velázquez, Rivera, and Torres, eds., *Revolution Around the Corner.*

[16] Ojeda Ríos was a Puerto Rican revolutionary killed by the FBI in a massive operation focused on his home in Hormigueros on September 23, 2005. An investigation by the Puerto Rico Civil Rights Commission completed in 2011 concluded that the operation "resulted in numerous human and civil rights violations" and was essentially illegal in nature.

[17] Rivera Ruiz, *Violencia Política y Subalternidad Colonial.*

[18] González Cruz, *Nacionalismo Revolucionario Puertorriqueño.*

[19] Enck-Wanzer, *The Young Lords: A Reader.*

[20] Meneses Albizu-Campos, *Una Vida de Amor y Sacrificio.*

[21] Doña Laura was essentially a biologist. Her bachelor's thesis was titled *The Physical-Chemical Process in Plant Inheritance.* Her doctoral thesis was titled *Contribution to the Study of Nitrification in the Soils of Lima.*

---

[22] Her granddaughter Cristina Meneses Albizu Campos wrote that Doña Laura often began to speak about her background by saying, "Nosotros, los indios."

[23] U.S. citizenship was imposed on all Puerto Ricans through the 1917 Jones Act.

[24] Laura de Albizu Campos, *Albizu Campos y la Independencia de Puerto Rico*.

[25] An offering given to God as part of a religious observance, also referring to the offering of bread and wine in the Eucharist.

[26] Rosado, *Las Llamas de la Aurora*.

[27] Rosario Natal, *Preso en Atlanta-Historia del Reo #51298-A (Correspondencia)*.

Afterword

I

According to Ruth Reynolds, a few days after the devastating San Ciriaco Hurricane finished passing over Puerto Rico in 1899, a young Don Pedro overheard remarks given by an officer of the U.S. Army that impacted him so much he remembered and recounted them years later to her. Commenting on the effects of the hurricane, the officer called it a godsend, saying that the U.S. government could not have gained so much economic control in such a short time without it. What followed were the formative years of the colonial regime that sectors of the Puerto Rican people opposed, but that would not be seriously challenged until thirty years later, in the 1930s, when Don Pedro led the Nationalist Party.

In September 2017, Puerto Rico endured two significant hurricanes in just two weeks. The second, Hurricane Maria, produced more than 4000 deaths, surpassing San Ciriaco's toll of over 3000. The entirety of Puerto Rico's infrastructure was severely damaged during Hurricane Maria, if not destroyed, and the collapse of the power grid left almost one hundred percent of the population without power for an entire year. When both the U.S. and colonial governments failed in their recovery efforts due to inaction and/or mismanagement, a national uproar followed. A renewed conversation regarding Puerto Rico's colonial status also developed.

Increasing numbers of people in Puerto Rico, and across the Puerto Rican diaspora, want to see the colonial status changed, and people are also becoming more engaged politically. In July 2019 the largest protests in Puerto Rican history took place. Besides lasting almost two weeks, they achieved their primary aim in what became the first time a governor in Puerto Rico resigned from their post. The mass exodus of Puerto Ricans as a result of the hurricanes, the rising impact of gentrification, and austerity measures brought about by La Junta, is high on the list of concerns for those interested in the future of Puerto Rico as a decolonized nation.

These times we are living in have even brought some to remember and repeat the words of Don Pedro. In 1933, still in the early stage of his political career, Don Pedro made a statement that Puerto Ricans needed to repatriate, because "spiritually, morally, many of you have been foreigners in Puerto Rico and unfortunately many Puerto Ricans do not feel Puerto Rican." Following his return from exile in 1947, Don Pedro's analysis of the situation in Puerto Rico changed as now the exodus was also physical. It was in this post-Operation Bootstrap climate of forced migration that Don Pedro made the prediction, if not prophecy, that many are recalling today due to the current context: "They want the cage, not the bird."

II

With the heightened discussion around Puerto Rico now taking place, it is an opportune time to learn about and reflect on the life and legacy of Don Pedro. This historical moment was not lost on me as I prepared to publish this book. In every conversation I had while completing the initial manuscript, I was reminded about its timeliness. While many of the reactions people shared with me pointed out values of the book that I was aware of, there were also many that I did not fully expect. Especially as I spoke with those Boricuas that hold a more active interest in their homeland's future, I was many times taken aback and humbled by the heartfelt and animated responses filled with gratitude that I received.

Making the first English-language biography of Puerto Rico's foremost nationalist leader available right now would have a tremendous impact on young Boricuas, many commented. This would be especially true for those Boricuas in the diaspora who are becoming increasingly English-dominant, and the countless numbers yet to be born to the victims of the contemporary forced migrations. On a few occasions I was told by parents that they would show the book to their children—one of these children, I was told, had Albizu as their middle name. This book, I was often reminded, would also serve to further teach the allies of Puerto Rico, who do not speak or read Spanish, about the colonial situation. This is true because when learning about Don Pedro one cannot avoid learning about this situation, and the resistance that has persisted in opposition to it.

There are many reasons this book deserved to be written. Hearing what others had to say about it before it was published was a profound experience. Of course, I also had my own reasons. As explained in the preface, before I even knew I would write this book I promised my father that I was going to publish something and that I would dedicate it to him— this book is the fulfillment of that promise. As a young adult I became an avid reader of Puerto Rican history and involved myself in honoring the Boricua diaspora and raising awareness around Puerto Rico's history—this book is an expression of my passions and personal commitments.

As a final comment, I cannot help but emphasize that I worked as tirelessly and carefully as I did on this book because of its potential historical and political value. Like my father before me, I hold the right of Puerto Rico to live out its future free of arbitrary, foreign rule as a non-negotiable. I do want independence for Puerto Rico. I would wager that many who picked up this book either felt the same way before reading its first pages, or that they now feel the same way as they read these last few. Such is usually the case when it comes to Don Pedro, for he both exemplifies the struggle for independence and powerfully articulated its ideals. I hope this book gets used in study groups, school programs, workshops, and other settings where our Boricua history is taught and discussed. I hope it inspires further work in support of the decolonization of Puerto Rico.

III

I feel that we cannot, and should not, overlook the fact that just when Don Pedro was close to securing the independence of Puerto Rico, in 1936, the U.S. government conspired to have him, and several other leaders imprisoned. This calculated repression of the independence movement by sectors of the U.S. government, which includes the killing of leaders and the infiltration and sabotage of organizations and movements, continued well after and into contemporary times. This history deserves a kind of restorative justice process where the stigma and misrepresentation of the independence movement and its ideals are reversed. Don Pedro started a similar project and became targeted with lethal repression as the leader of a movement it was felt could seriously threaten U.S. control in Puerto Rico.

In closing, I'm reminded of something a nationalist told me about the struggle for independence during a trip to Lares more than a decade ago. Referring to the population size of Puerto Rico at the time—almost four million—they told me: "We don't need another Albizu. We need four million Albizus. We need every Puerto Rican to have that level of consciousness and sense of *valor y sacrificio*." Thirty-one years passed between Hurricane San Ciriaco and Don Pedro emerging as the president of the Nationalist Party. It's been over four years since Hurricane Maria. Many developments have taken place in Puerto Rico, but underneath it all, the colonial status of the archipelago remains unchanged.

Are we in another critical moment with the potential to change Puerto Rico forever? Many feel that we are. As we draw lessons from history, tap into the technologies and resources that the age we live in affords us, and build the organizational and solidarity networks, with the involvement of the ever-growing Boricua diaspora, that a decolonized Puerto Rico will need, may the life and legacy of Don Pedro inspire us all and the work that continues...

References

Books:

Acosta, Ivonne. *La Palabra Como Delito: Los Discursos por los que Condenaron a Pedro Albizu Campos 1948-1950*. Editorial Cultural, 1993.

Acosta Lespier, Ivonne. *La Mordaza (The Gag Law): The Attempt To Crush The Independence Movement In Puerto Rico (1948-1957)*. DS Editores, 2018.

Albizu-Campos Meneses, Laura and Fr. Rodríguez León, Mario A. O.P., eds. *Pedro Albizu Campos: Escritos*. Publicaciones Puertorriqueñas, 2007.

Aponte Vázquez, Pedro. *Locura Por Decreto: El Papel De Luis Muñoz Marín Y José Trías Monge En El Diagnóstico De Locura De Don Pedro Albizu Campos*. 2005.

Aponte Vázquez, Pedro. *¡Yo Acuso! Y Lo Que Pasó Después*. 2009.

Badillo, Jalil Sued. *Agüeybaná El Bravo: La Recuperación De Un Símbolo*. Ediciones Puerto, 2008.

Baralt, Guillermo A. *Slave Revolts In Puerto Rico: Conspiracies And Uprisings, 1795-1873*. Markus Wiener Publishers, 2007.

Corretjer, Juan Antonio. *La Lucha por la Independencia de Puerto Rico*. Liga Socialista Puertorriqueña, *1949*.

de Albizu Campos, Laura. *Albizu Campos y la Independencia de Puerto Rico*. Publicaciones Puertorriqueñas, 2007.

Denis, Nelson A. *War Against All Puerto Ricans: Revolution and Terror In America's Colony*. Nation Books, 2015.

Enck-Wanzer, Darrel, ed. *The Young Lords: A Reader*. New York University Press, 2010.

González Cruz, Michael. *Nacionalismo Revolucionario Puertorriqueño: La Lucha Armada, Intelectuales y Prisioneros Políticos y de Guerra (1956-2005)*. Editorial Isla Negra, 2018.

Jiménez de Wagenheim, Olga. *Nationalist Heroines: Puerto Rican Women History Forgot, 1930s-1950s*. Markus Wiener Publishers, 2016.

Jiménez de Wagenheim, Olga. *Puerto Rico's Revolt For Independence: El Grito De Lares*. Markus Wiener Publishers, 1997.

Mari Brás, Juan. *El Independentismo En Puerto Rico: Su Pasado, Su Presente Y Su Porvenir*. Editorial Cepa, 1984.

Medina Ramírez, Ramón. *El Movimiento Libertador en la Historia de Puerto Rico*. San Juan, Puerto Rico, 1970.

Meneses Albizu-Campos, Cristina. *La Espiritualidad de Pedro Albizu Campos*. Publicaciones Puertorriqueñas, 2008.

Meneses Albizu-Campos, Cristina. *Una Vida de Amor y Sacrificio*. Publicaciones Puertorriqueñas, 2009.

Meyer, Gerald. *Vito Marcantonio: Radical Politician 1902-1954*. State University of New York Press, 1989.

Negroni, Héctor Andrés. *Historia Militar de Puerto Rico*. Sociedad Estatal Quinto Centenario, 1992.

Paralitici, Ché. *Sentencia Impuesta: 100 Años de Encarcelamientos por la Independencia de Puerto Rico*. Ediciones Puerto, 2004.

Rivera Ruiz, Álvaro M. *Violencia Política y Subalternidad Colonial: El Caso de Filiberto Ojeda y el MIRA (1960-1972)*. Centro de Estudios Avanzados de Puerto Rico y el Caribe, 2020.

Rosado, Marisa. *El Nacionalismo y la Violencia en la Década de 1930*. Ediciones Puerto, 2007.

Rosado, Marisa. *Pedro Albizu Campos: Las Llamas de la Aurora-Acercamiento a su Biografía*. Ediciones Puerto, 2008.

Rosario Natal, Carmelo. *Albizu Campos: Preso en Atlanta-Historia del Reo #51298-A (Correspondencia)*. Producciones Históricas, 2001.

Rouse, Irving. *The Tainos: Rise and Decline of the People Who Greeted Columbus*. Yale University Press, 1992.

Rubenstein, Annette, ed. *I Vote My Conscience: Debates, Speeches, and Writings of Vito Marcantonio*. A. M. Kelley, 1973.

Seijo Bruno, Miñi. *La Insurrección Nacionalista en Puerto Rico 1950*. Editorial Edil, 1997.

Silén, Juan Angel. *Nosotros Solos: Pedro Albizu Campos y el Nacionalismo Irlandés*. Publicaciones Gaviotas, 2003.

Stevens-Arroyo, Antonio M. *Cave of the Jagua: The Mythological World of the Taínos*. University of Scranton Press, 2006.

Torres, J. Benjamín, ed. *Pedro Albizu Campos: Obras Escogidas, 1923-1936, Tomo I*. Editorial Jelofe, 1975.

Torres, J. Benjamín, ed. *Pedro Albizu Campos: Obras Escogidas, 1923-1936, Tomo II*. Editorial Jelofe, 1981.

Torres, J. Benjamín, ed. *Pedro Albizu Campos: Obras Escogidas, 1923-1936, Tomo III*. Editorial Jelofe, 1981.

Velázquez, José E., Rivera, Carmen V., and Torres, Andrés, eds. *Revolution Around the Corner: Voices from the Puerto Rican Socialist Party in the U.S.*. Temple University Press, 2020.

Wilson, Samuel M. *The Archaeology of the Caribbean*. Cambridge University Press, 2007.

Pamphlets and Articles:

"Bright Idea: The First Lasers." American Institute of Physics.

"El Dr. Manuel de la Pila Iglesias: Ilustre médico de Ponce y Puerto Rico." *Galenus* Vol. 9.

Frédéric and Irène Joliot-Curie: French Chemists. Encyclopædia Britannica, Inc., 2021.

Acosta Lespier, Ivonne. "La 'Transfiguración Gloriosa De La Patria' De Acuerdo A Pedro Albizu Campos." Sin Mordazas Blog, 2013.

Corretjer, Juan Antonio. *Albizu Campos and the Ponce Massacre.* World View Forum, 1992.

Dr. Franqui-Rivera, Harry. "The Porto Rican Division." *The Puerto Rican Experience In The U.S. Military: A Century Of Unheralded Service.* Center for Puerto Rican Studies.

Partido Nacionalista De Puerto Rico. *Plantao En La Revolución.* Ediciones Año Pre-Centenario De La Proclamación De La República, 1967.

Torres, J. Benjamín. *El Proceso Judicial Contra Pedro Albizu Campos En El 1936.* Editorial Jelofe, 1974.

Academic Essays:

Dávila, José Manuel. *Metamorfosis: de las Hijas de la Libertad al Cuerpo de Enfermerade la República del Partido Nacionalista de Puerto Rico, 1932-1937.* Asociación Puertorriqueña de Investigación de Historia de las Mujeres.

De Jesús, Anthony. "I have endeavored to seize the beautiful opportunity for learning offered here: Pedro Albizu Campos at Harvard a century ago." *Latino Studies* 9 (2011).

Delgado Cintrón, Carmelo. "El Derecho En Pedro Albizu Campos: La Formación Jurídica." In *La Nación Puertorriqueña: Ensayos En Torno A Pedro*

Albizu Campos. Universidad de Puerto Rico, 1997.

Estades-Font , María E. "The Critical Year of 1936 through the Reports of the Military Intelligence Division." In *Puerto Rico Under Colonial Rule: Political Persecution and the Quest for Human Rights*. State University of New York Press: Albany, 2006.

Sánchez Huertas, Ernesto. "Algunas Ideas Tentativas del Pensamiento Social Cristiano en Pedro Albizu Campos." In *La Nación Puertorriqueña: Ensayos En Torno A Pedro Albizu Campos*. Universidad de Puerto Rico, 1997.

Stevens-Arroyo, Anthony M. "The Catholic Worldview in the Political Philosophy of Pedro Albizu Campos: The Death Knoll of Puerto Rican Insularity." *U.S. Catholic Historian* 21, 4 (Fall 2002).

Tirado Avilés, Amílcar. "La Forja de un Líder: Pedro Albizu Campos, 1924-1930." In *La Nación Puertorriqueña: Ensayos En Torno A Pedro Albizu Campos*. Universidad de Puerto Rico, 1997.

News Articles:

"Assassin's Boasts Trapped Suspects; Arrests in New York Followed Collazo Bragging, Grand Jury Witness Says." *The New York Times*, 10 November 1950.

"Ausubo Press will Publish Ireland and Puerto Rico: The Untold Story by Aoife Rivera Serrano ." *PR Web*, 2009.

"Commutation Approved." *The New York Times*, 26 July 1952.

"Cosmopolitan Club Plans for "International Night" Feb. 21." *The Harvard Crimson*, 25 January 1919.

"Dr. Rhoads Cleared of Porto Rico Plot; Letter Telling of Giving Cancer to Natives Is Declared to Have Been Parody. Incident Held Closed. Governor Accepts Findings of Medical Association, Health Commissioner and Attorney General." *The New York Times*, 15 February 1932.

"Forum Decided Against Giving Aid To Allies." *The Harvard Crimson*, 11 November 1915.

"Island Rebels Ask U.N. To Investigate; Aide Of Puerto Rico Nationalists Deposits Request For Study Of Revolt As Threat To Peace." *The New York Times*, 3 November 1950.

"Mob Invades New Capitol of Porto Rico; Youth Killed in Riot Over Flag for Island; Mob Raids Capitol In Porto Rico Riot." *The New York Times*, 18 April 1932.

"Regiment Commander Gave Detailed Plans." *The Harvard Crimson*, 05 January 1916.

"R.O.T.C. Training Completed Successfully At Barre." *The Harvard Crimson*, 21 September 1917.

"Training Corps Is Officially Established." *The Harvard Crimson*, 08 February 1917.

"University Regiment Officially Approved." *The Harvard Crimson*, 12 February 1916.

"Voluntary Military Drill." *The Harvard Crimson*, 30 November 1915.

"Win Puerto Rican Trial; Albizu and Portilla Are Freed of Capitol Riot Charge." *The New York Times*, 24 June 1932.

Acevedo, Nicole. "Puerto Rico Sees More Pain And Little Progress Three Years After Hurricane Maria." *NBC News*, 20 September 2020.

Albizu Campos, Pedro. "Porto Rico and the War." *The Harvard Crimson*, 14 April 1917.

IPS Correspondents. "Rights: Group Strips Racist Scientist's Name from Award." *Inter Press Service*, 29 April 2003.

Archival References:

1910 United States Federal Census. Accessed on Ancestry.com.

New York, U.S., Arriving Passenger and Crew Lists (including Castle Garden and Ellis Island), 1820-1957. Accessed on Ancestry.com.

Puerto Rico, Civil Registrations, 1885-2001. Accessed on Ancestry.com.

Puerto Rico, Registro Central de Esclavos, 1872. Accessed on Ancestry.com.

Puerto Rico, U.S, Arriving Passenger and Crew Lists, 1901-1962. Accessed on Ancestry.com.

Center for Puerto Rican Studies Library and Archives. *Historical Journals and Periodicals.* Hunter College, CUNY.

Center for Puerto Rican Studies Library and Archives. *The Ruth M. Reynolds Papers.* Hunter College, CUNY.

Other References:

Chapter XI: Declaration Regarding Non-Self-Governing Territories. Charter Of The United Nations.

The Harvard Graduates' Magazine, Volume XXV. 1916-1917. The Harvard Graduates' Magazine Association, 1917.

Aponte Vázquez, Pedro. *Los Últimos Días De Don Pedro Albizu Campos.* 2012.

whoisalbizu. "Interview with José Enrique Ayoroa Santaliz, Episode 1: Albizu's Birthday." YouTube video, 2011.

whoisalbizu. "Interview with José Enrique Ayoroa Santaliz, Episode 2: El Maestro." YouTube video, 2011.

Published July 14, 2022
ISBN: 978-0-578-29275-5

CPSIA information can be obtained
at www.ICGtesting.com
Printed in the USA
LVHW102000300822
727188LV00004B/98

9 780578 292755